HANNIBAL

ROME'S GREATEST ENEMY

Soldiers have so much to learn by studying the ancients ... those same principles of war that applied to the days of Hannibal apply today.
Norman Schwarzkopf

Hannibal's enduring reputation as a man and as a general is due to his enemies' fascination with him. The way his legend was shaped in the Greek and Roman consciousness is one of the book's main themes.

Under Hannibal's leadership, Carthage came close to dominating the western Mediterranean. That he was a brilliant general is unquestioned, yet his political career is less appreciated and his achievements as civilian leader of Carthage in 196–5 BC have been virtually overlooked. The issues of whether he might indeed have changed history had he postponed conflict with Rome, and what he did achieve for Carthage in the end, are explored in this volume as vigorously as the military questions.

Dexter Hoyos is retired Associate Professor of Latin in the University of Sydney and author of *Unplanned Wars: the Origins of the First and Second Punic Wars* (1998), *Hannibal's Dynasty: Power and Politics in the Western Mediterranean, 247–183 BC* (2003), and *Truceless War: Carthage's Fight for Survival, 241–237 BC* (2007).

GREECE AND ROME LIVE

Also available in this series:
Ancient Greece in Film and Popular Culture, Gideon Nisbet (2006; second edition 2008)
Augustine: The Confessions, Gillian Clark (2005)
Gruesome Deaths and Celibate Lives: Christian Martyrs and Ascetics, Aideen M. Hartney (2005)
Hadrian's Wall and its People, Geraint Osborn (2006)
Julius Caesar, Robert Garland (2004)
The Politics of Greek Tragedy, David M. Carter (2007)
Reading Catullus, John Godwin (2008)
The Tragedies of Sophocles, James Morwood (2008)

Forthcoming titles:
After Virgil: The Poetry, Politics and Perversion of Roman Epic, Robert Cowan
Ancient Rome at the Cinema: Story and Spectacle in Hollywood and Rome, Elena Theodorakopoulos
Augustus: Caesar's Web: Power and Propaganda in Augustan Rome, Matthew D.H. Clark
The Classical Greek House, Janett Morgan
Greek Tyranny, Sian Lewis
The Law in Ancient Greece, Christopher Carey
Pausanias: An Ancient Guide to Greece, John Taylor
The Trojan War, Emma Stafford

HANNIBAL
ROME'S GREATEST ENEMY

Dexter Hoyos

BRISTOL
PHOENIX
PRESS

First published in 2008 by
Bristol Phoenix Press
an imprint of The Exeter Press
Reed Hall, Streatham Drive
Exeter, Devon EX4 4QR
UK
www.exeterpress.co.uk

Every effort has been made to contact copyright holders in order to obtain
permission for use of the illustrations. We would like to take this opportunity to
acknowledge any copyright holder that we may have failed to contact.

British Library Cataloguing in Publication Data
A catalogue record for this book is available from the British Library

Paperback ISBN 13: 978 1 904675 47 1
Hardback ISBN 13: 978 1 904675 46 4

Typeset by Carnegie Book Production, Lancaster in Chaparral Pro 11pt on 15pt
Printed in Great Britain by CPI Antony Rowe, Chippenham

Some regard him as having been extraordinarily cruel, some exceedingly grasping of money. Fond of money indeed he does seem to have been to a conspicuous degree, [but] who could refrain from speaking in terms of admiration of this great man's strategic skill, courage, and ability, when one looks to the length of time during which he displayed those qualities? ... For sixteen continuous years Hannibal maintained the war with Rome in Italy, without once releasing his army from service in the field. There can be no fear in saying that, if he had reserved his attack upon the Romans until he had first subdued other parts of the world, there is not one of his projects which would have eluded his grasp.

Polybius 9.24–25, 11.19 (tr. E.S. Shuckburgh)

Hannibal was possessed of enormous daring in facing dangers, and enormous resourcefulness when in the midst of those dangers. He could be physically exhausted or mentally cowed by no hardship. ... Only the time he had left from discharging his duties was given to sleep ... On horse or foot he was far the best soldier; the first to enter battle, he was the last to leave once battle was joined. [Yet] the man's great virtues were matched by his enormous vices: pitiless cruelty, a treachery worse than Punic, no regard for truth and no integrity, no fear of the gods or respect for an oath, and no scruples.

Livy 21.4 (tr. J.C. Yardley)

He could comprehend matters most clearly and plan out most promptly every project that he conceived, notwithstanding the fact that, as a rule, sureness is the result of deliberation and instability the result of a hasty disposition. He was most resourceful in the suddenest emergency, and most steadfast to the point of utter trustworthiness. Not only did he safely handle the affair of the moment, but he accurately read the future beforehand. Consequently he, above all other men, met each occasion with suitable words and acts, because he viewed the expected and the actual in the same light.

Dio, fragment 54, tr. E. Cary

CONTENTS

ILLUSTRATIONS

Cover illustration (paperback): 'Hannibal crossing the Alps' (and losing elephants): print by Heinrich Leutemann (1862). Everything is happening at once: exhausted troops, collapsing pack-animals, plunging elephants, hostile Gauls and, seemingly, Hannibal pointing the way to Italy.

PREFACE

Hannibal's inclusion in *Greece & Rome Live* is well merited. As one of the ancient world's three leading commanders, and the leader of a republic which in his day matched Rome and the Greek world in dynamism, wealth and potential, he was rightly remembered by both Romans and Greeks as an equal. Carthage was far from being an enclosed and self-absorbed community of Near Easterners exotically planted in Africa. She was energetically outward-looking, her culture constantly evolving and – by his time – more and more attuned to Hellenistic Greek civilisation. Rome was undergoing the same process. Nor was it a contest of Punic David versus Roman Goliath, as the story will show. Hannibal's War was an epic struggle between two powers more similar to each other than is usually thought.

Hannibal's life is told to us entirely by non-Carthaginians. Many Greek and Roman accounts, moreover, are preserved only in part. Even so, the qualities of his leadership, the fascination of his exploits, and some glimpses of his own personality are vividly reported with a blend of hostility and admiration; their accounts, indeed, are at times less critical of him than they could be (as again this story will show). For all these reasons, Hannibal's career is filled with events and issues which remain sharply debated, and often explained in contradictory ways, by historians: from his boyhood oath to the tantalising questions of whether he could really have won, and what the effect on history would have been. This book offers answers that may, in places, surprise.

HANNIBAL'S CHRONOLOGY

All dates BC

247   Hamilcar Barca appointed general in Sicily against Romans. Hannibal born.

241   End of First Punic War, on Roman terms

241 (end)–237 (early) 'Truceless War' in North Africa, won for Carthage by Hamilcar. Barcid political dominance at Carthage begins. Hamilcar, with eldest son Hannibal, leads expedition to Spain

237–229/8 (winter)   Hamilcar establishes Carthaginian dominion in southern Spain. Killed on campaign

229/8–221 (autumn)   Hasdrubal, Hamilcar's son-in-law, as new general further extends Punic rule. (± 227) founds Spanish Carthage (New Carthage to Romans)

221   Hannibal elected new general on Hasdrubal's assassination

219   Hannibal besieges and sacks Saguntum (April–November)

218–216   Outbreak of Second Punic War. Hannibal invades Italy. Victories at river Trebia (*c.* 22 December 218), Lake Trasimene (21 June 217) and Cannae (2 August 216)

218–211   Elder Scipio brothers campaign in Spain

215–212   Most of southern Italy joins Hannibal's side, notably
            Capua (215) and Tarentum (212). Romans wage
            defensive war under guidance of Fabius the Delayer,
            Claudius Marcellus and others

214   Syracuse joins war on Carthaginian side

212   Capua besieged. First battle of Herdonea. Marcellus
            takes Syracuse

211   Roman forces in Spain annihilated. Hannibal's March
            on Rome fails. Capua surrenders to Romans

210   Second battle of Herdonea. Battle of Numistro

209   New Roman commander in Spain, Publius Scipio
            the younger, seizes New Carthage. Fabius recaptures
            Tarentum

208   Death of Marcellus in ambush in Apulia

208–206   Scipio's victories at Baecula and Ilipa destroy
            Carthaginian power in Spain

207   Invasion of Italy by Hannibal's brother Hasdrubal
            destroyed at River Metaurus

206–203   Hannibal on defensive in southern Italy. (206)
            Hannibal sets up record of his campaigns at Cape
            Lacinium

205   Scipio's consulship. Hannibal's brother Mago invades
            Liguria (N. Italy)

204   Scipio invades North Africa

203   Scipio's victories in North Africa. He makes Masinissa
            king of Numidia (reign, 203–149). Peace made with
            Carthage but then broken. Defeat and death of Mago.
            Hannibal returns to Africa after 34 years

202   Battle of Zama (*c.* 19 October)

201   Peace treaty, effectively disarming Carthage

196   Hannibal holds office of sufete, reforms politics and
            finances

195   Hannibal forced into exile, with Roman connivance

195–189   Hannibal at the court of the Great King, Antiochus III

189–187/6   Hannibal at the court of Artaxias of Armenia

187/6–183   Hannibal at the court of Prusias of Bithynia

183 (or early 182)   Suicide of Hannibal

149–146   Third Punic War and sack of Carthage

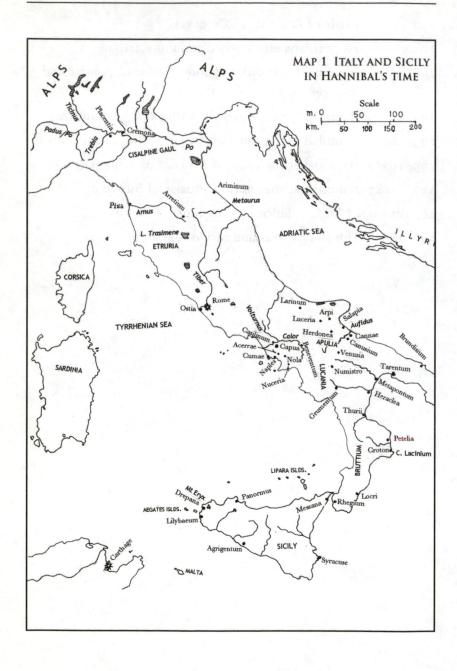

MAP 1 ITALY AND SICILY
IN HANNIBAL'S TIME

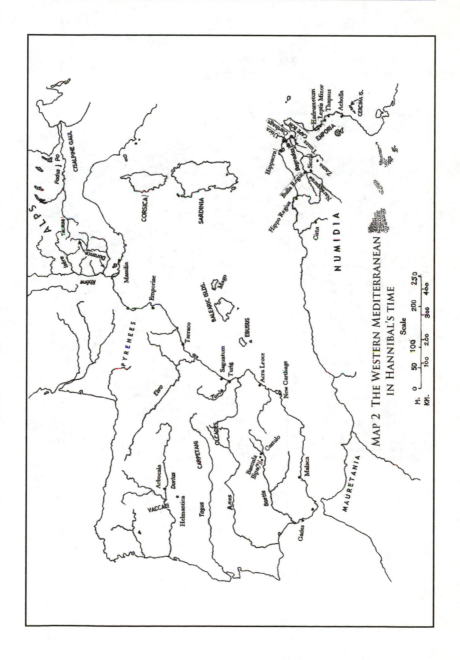

MAP 2 THE WESTERN MEDITERRANEAN IN HANNIBAL'S TIME

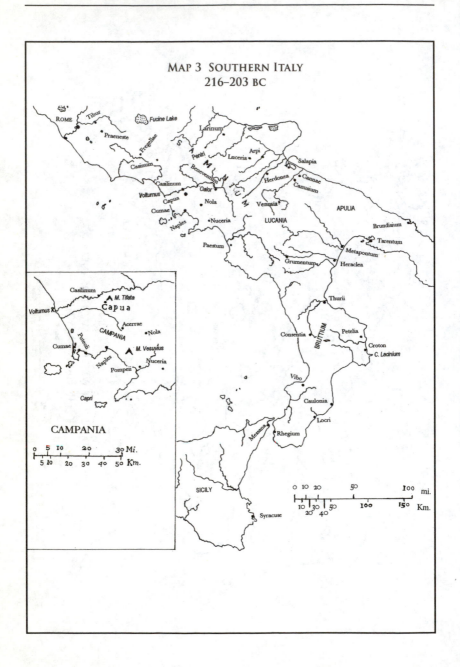

MAP 3 SOUTHERN ITALY
216–203 BC

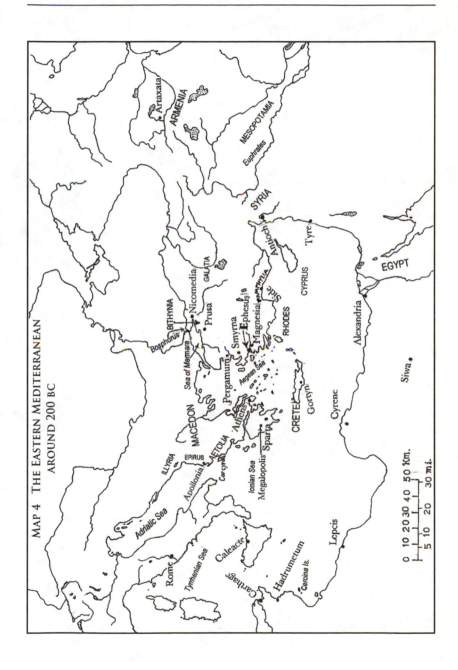

MAP 4   THE EASTERN MEDITERRANEAN
AROUND 200 BC

CHAPTER 1

INTRODUCTION
THE CHALLENGE OF HANNIBAL

H annibal excited, frightened and – once safely dead – drew reluctant admiration from the Romans. They accused him of treachery, cruelty, greed and unreasoning hatred; at the same time they recognised his inspired leadership, military genius, and tireless resourcefulness. Uneasily, too, they remembered that they had hounded him to his death.

Hannibal is one of a trio of generals whom later ages acclaimed as the greatest in the ancient world, with Alexander before him and Caesar after. In many ways he was untypical. He was neither a Greek nor a Roman; he did not command a national army although he was a national leader; he conquered no lasting territory and lost his greatest war; he was exiled from home; and his fame has been perpetuated by his enemies. His personal life is barely known, but like Alexander and Caesar he was an inspired battlefield commander, a resourceful strategist and an inspiration to both his troops and his countrymen. He expanded Alexander's flexibility of manoeuvre to develop tactics still studied, and used, today. And, like Caesar, he later carried out constructive reforms at home which made a lasting impact on his city's politics and prosperity.

Posterity, Roman and later, has cherished a classic image – the charismatic general on an elephant at the crest of the Alps, pointing out to his weary men the road to Italy. This tableau of Hannibal, tropical elephants and snow-covered mountains remains the most popular idea of him. Ironically, it has little to do with his achievements. Elephants played only a small part in his battles (arguably, they gave more trouble than use), while the Alpine crossing was a near-disaster for his broader strategy. His achievement as general was to rise above these limitations, make Carthage for a decade the principal power in the West, and come tantalisingly close to establishing her, instead of Rome, as the fulcrum of future history.

This was, it seems, his goal. He made it clear that he judged the struggle with Rome as a war not to the death, but for honour and supremacy. The glimpses we have of how he envisaged the Mediterranean world after final victory are of Carthage dominant over the West – including Rome – and on equal terms with the great powers of the Hellenistic East; but with the Romans still a power requiring surveillance. How he would have managed such a geopolitical system makes for interesting speculation. How and why fortune refused him victory – and how much he himself contributed to this – are even more interesting questions.

Modern fascinations with Hannibal follow three broad paths. There is the individualist hero with his elephants, a picture essentially one-dimensional but malleable for novels and films. Another, more specialised and analytical, focuses on the military genius and master of the battlefield. This is the Hannibal most widely studied: it is not by chance that most books devote as much (or more) space to his epic invasion march and the ensuing three great victories as to the rest of his quite long life. A third approach, crucial though less widespread, focuses on him as architect of grand strategy, geopolitics and even cultural assertion – for instance, as a champion of democracy against the oligarchic oppression of Rome.

Some though not all of these aspects are well founded, but Hannibal's historical importance involves other features again. He inherited and furthered Carthage's remarkable recovery from the ravages of earlier wars. He led the Carthaginians in the most powerful challenge made to the rising Roman state since marauding Gauls had sacked the city nearly two centuries earlier, and the last life-or-death challenge for five hundred years. He proved the potential of a fully multicultural Mediterranean empire and army – a potential which, ironically, his Roman enemies would harness. He revealed too the resilient vigour of the peoples of North Africa, who, in the shape of his Punic and Numidian descendants, would in turn contribute decisively to Roman civilisation. The Carthaginians' decade-long predominance in western Mediterranean affairs, from 218 to 207 BC, was his doing, as the mediocre quality of all the other Punic leaders of the time confirms.

All these achievements were accompanied and, in the end, were overturned partly by circumstances beyond his control and partly – but significantly – by mistakes and miscalculations that were his own. In turn, his and his city's defeat (no matter what the qualities of the Romans' later opponents) assured to Rome the inevitability of tricontinental empire. Even so, after defeat he set his homeland again on the road to prosperity and, this time, to a measure of democracy as well – a success which, ironically and tragically, would secure the destruction of Carthage after his death.

The sources for Hannibal

Remarkably, no record of Hannibal by a Carthaginian or pro-Carthaginian writer survives, though we know that several were written. He himself described his Italian campaigns in an inscription set up in a seaside temple in southern Italy. Two Greek literary and academic friends of his, named Silenus and Sosylus, accompanied him over most of his active life and then composed accounts of his doings. But apart from the text of Hannibal's treaty in 215 with Philip V of Macedon, quoted by Polybius, and a piece of papyrus with Sosylus' narrative of a Spanish sea-battle, nothing remains of these works outside references in surviving writers. The same holds for two Roman contemporaries of Hannibal, Fabius Pictor and Cincius Alimentus, whose histories of Rome, in Greek, went down to the Second Punic War (Cincius had conversed with Hannibal himself after becoming a prisoner of war), and for Cato the Censor (234–149), another veteran of the war who, late in life, composed the first history in Latin. Nor do the many second-century and early first-century works that included the war and its aftermath survive; among them the first historical monograph in Latin, written some time after 120 by Coelius Antipater, who combined a measure of literary elegance with conscientious if not always first-rate research.

Of the surviving accounts, nearest to Hannibal's time is the history of the Mediterranean world by Polybius (c. 200–118), a distinguished Greek from Megalopolis in the Peloponnese, whose forty detailed books covered the era from 264 to the destruction of Carthage in 146. Like most lengthy ancient works, we do not have all of it – only the first five books, taking the story down to Cannae in 216, and then numerous extracts from the rest. With few literary pretensions (these did not interest the author) it is, nonetheless, one of the most masterful achievements of ancient historiography. Polybius was perceptive, analytical and sceptical; he sought out eyewitnesses on both sides of events, and likewise read widely and variedly. His eminence in the Achaean League, to which Megalopolis belonged, brought him direct experience of military and political affairs. An enforced seventeen-year exile at Rome gave him a strong, but tempered, admiration for the Romans and, at the same time, a rational respect for the qualities of their leading opponents – notably Hannibal. Despite a lofty opinion of his own talents, and intermittent vaguenesses even on military matters (his account of Hannibal's Alpine march is even less detailed than the Roman historian Livy's, for instance), he is the single most important authority we have on Hannibal's achievements as a general.

The fullest narrative to survive is by Livy (Titus Livius, 64 BC–AD 12), who wrote a detailed history of Rome from its foundation (its title is *From the Foundation of the City*) to his own day, in 142 books. While only thirty-five remain, these include Books 21 to 45 on events from 219 to 167. Hannibal is a dominating figure in Livy's narrative of the Second Punic War (Books 21–30), along with outstanding Roman leaders such as Fabius the Delayer, the pugnacious Marcus Marcellus and, finally, Hannibal's nemesis, Scipio Africanus. The Carthaginian then reappears in later books until Livy records his suicide in Book 39. Livy's account, in fact, is the nearest substitute we have for a large-scale biography. His historical and analytical skills were limited – his considerable genius was literary, his enthusiasm patriotic – but he consulted a range of sources, notably Polybius and probably also Silenus and Sosylus, and made diligent efforts to arrive at the truth or, at least, likelihood.

To his narrative and that of Polybius our other extant sources variously add some confirmations, extra items, or contradictions (most of them implausible). Cornelius Nepos (*c*. 110–24 BC), an acquaintance of Cicero's, wrote a very short biography of Hannibal which, interestingly, draws in part on sources friendly to him, and covers his life after the war in several paragraphs. Nepos also put together a three-paragraph sketch of Hamilcar Barca. Then in Augustus' time a Gallic-born writer, Pompeius Trogus, wrote a history of the world – Rome excepted – which survives in a later epitome by one Justin; it has a few items on Hannibal's life as an exile that match details in Nepos and Livy. Two other large histories in Greek survive, but only in extracts, for Hannibal's time: a world history by Diodorus, of the later first century BC, which includes Roman affairs; and a general history of Rome down to his own time by Cassius Dio, a distinguished senator and consul (AD 164–c. 240). Diodorus' few remaining extracts on Hannibal's era rely, partly anyway, on a well-informed predecessor or predecessors, so the loss of the rest is all the more unfortunate. Of Dio's history of this period, only some excerpts and a medieval Byzantine précis survive, again a pity since Dio read widely in earlier works and had some independence of judgement.

The philosophic writer Plutarch (c. AD 46–120) and Appian, a retired bureaucrat of the late second century AD, did write works in Greek that survive. Two of Plutarch's famous *Lives*, on Hannibal's opponents Fabius the Delayer and Claudius Marcellus, have much to report on Hannibal, whom the biographer treats fairly objectively. Appian is – or could have been – more useful still, for his narratives on the wars of the Roman republic include one (called *Hannibalica*) on Hannibal's Italian campaigns, while Scipio's in Africa are in the first part of *Libyca*, and his *Iberica*, on the Romans' wars in Spain, naturally reports their Second Punic War operations there. Yet in these narratives Appian repeatedly disappoints. Where they contradict details in Polybius and Livy they rarely deserve preference – for example, when he reports for Cannae actions that we know happened at the Trebia, and when he makes Hannibal and Scipio clash heroically and fictitiously hand-to-hand at Zama. Appian also shows a dubious grasp of geography – confusing Saguntum (Sagunto near Valencia) with New Carthage (Cartagena), for instance – and a propensity to exaggerate numbers. He is much better on the Third Punic War of 149–146, for which he draws on a high-quality source, probably Polybius. By contrast, Hannibalic-era details of his, if not corroborated by other writers, need to be assessed with care.

Many other ancient writers contribute scattered items on Hannibal and his city. For instance, Livy's close contemporary, the geographer Strabo, rather briefly describes North Africa and Carthage itself; one Valerius Maximus in the 30s AD collected moralising historical anecdotes, many of them of Hannibalic War episodes; and around AD 100 Frontinus, an eminent former consul and governor of Britain, compiled a handbook of past military stratagems, again with Hannibalic items. From the later fourth century AD we have Eutropius' very short epitome of Roman history, and from around AD 420 a pious history 'against the pagans' compiled by a Spanish churchman, Orosius, to show that fifth-century barbarian invasions were far less deplorable than past catastrophes. Meanwhile, in a class of its own – scarcely usable as history apart from two or three possible nuggets, despite occasional scholarly efforts to locate more – is *Punica*, a 17-book epic poem on Hannibal's war by Silius Italicus, an ex-consul and poet (AD 26–101), who offers a necessarily episodic version of the war in grandiose style, with individual heroic combats, cliché-ridden speeches, and the usual divine interferences.

Archaeology and documentary materials do not contribute a great deal, and some of their evidence is debated. For instance, finely made coins from Punic Spain, with Greek-style portraits in profile, are often thought to portray Hannibal as leader, as well as his two predecessors, but this has been contested. A group of burial pits near the northern shore of Lake Trasimene has, similarly, been both claimed and rejected for that battle-site. Uncontroversial and appealing is the epitaph of an Etruscan named Felsnas Larth, who lived to be 106 and whose proudest deeds, as his tomb-epitaph at Tarquinii records, were that 'he sojourned at Capua and fought together with Hannibal's people'.[1]

Most controversial of all is the famous pair of recessed artificial harbours, commercial and naval, on the southern flank of Carthage itself: a rectangular outer one for merchant shipping, the circular inner one for the navy. Although today in very run-down condition, they are extensively described by Appian in his account of the Third Punic War, probably drawing on Polybius as noted above. When were these havens built? Very little evidence from the sites predates the 150s. Yet after 201 the Carthaginians were forbidden to have a navy and, therefore, had no need of an expensive port to house and supply two hundred warships. If the ports date to Barcid times instead, they raise other difficult questions, as we shall see.

Modern historians often look sceptically on the idea of studying a subject for which almost all the available materials date from 50 to 650 years later. Hannibal is a peculiarly difficult case since none of the written records is, strictly speaking, Carthaginian. Yet it can be shown that pro-Carthaginian as well as anti-Carthaginian sources are reflected in what survives; while even the most patriotic Roman writers – Livy most strikingly – were prepared to admit some constructive qualities in their most memorable foe. Thus, in spite of the limitations on what we can know, a coherent historical portrait can still be drawn of the only Carthaginian whose name remains a household word today.

CHAPTER 2

FAMILY AND CITY

The republic of Carthage

The first Carthaginians to settle the arrow-shaped promontory with its commanding Byrsa hill had been Phoenicians from Tyre, under their legendary queen Dido and traditionally in 813. The Romans' dates for their own city varied between 753 and 747, which put the two foundations barely a couple of generations apart in age; and, as it happened, Roman legend alleged eastern ancestors too – refugees from Troy led by Aeneas, whose descendants Romulus and Remus, 400 years later, would found the city on seven hills. Grandly ignoring chronology, all the same, Virgil's *Aeneid* brings together Aeneas himself and Dido in a passionate love affair which ends tragically, with the deserted queen calling down a curse – and a future avenger, clearly implying Hannibal – on his descendants.

There were other Phoenician colonies in the area: notably Utica a few hours' sail to the north, Hippacra (modern Bizerte) a further day's sail up the coast, and Hadrumetum and Leptis Minor (Sousse and Lamta) to the south-east by the Gulf of Sirte. Some were older than Dido's 'New City', hence its name: Qart-Hadasht in the Punic language. Close relations were maintained with Tyre, but Phoenicia could not supply an endless stream of settlers. Intermarriage with native Libyans was no doubt frequent, as well as with Numidians from further west (we know of several examples, including two of Hannibal's sisters), and unions with Sicilian Greeks and with Spaniards are also recorded. The Carthaginians were therefore a multi-ethnic people, an issue of no interest to Greeks and Romans, who themselves had a fine range of backgrounds. What mattered was cultural identity. Hannibal's people spoke a form of Phoenician called Punic; they worshipped Phoenician divinities such as Ba'al Hammon, his consort Tanit, Melqart the city's protecting deity, and Eshmun whose temple crowned the Byrsa hill where the Cathedral of St Louis stands today. They decorated their buildings and homes with stucco and distinctive floor-pavings which the Romans were to call *pavimenta Punica*; and, as ritual dedications to the gods, crafted bronze hatchet-shaped razors with fine pictorial engravings.

At the same time, Carthaginian culture was not static or introverted. If they ever practised child- or infant-sacrifice, as some ancient writers claim and as evidence from the sacred cemetery, in the southern part of the city, is alleged to confirm (although there is much dispute about this), they had ceased the rite well before Hannibal's time. Over the centuries they borrowed or adapted features from elsewhere, such as art-styles from Egypt and, from the Greeks, features of architecture, art, coinage and religion – such as the cult of Demeter and Persephone, ceremoniously adopted in 396. Peristyles in houses, fine statuary (some of it plundered from Sicilian cities), building-decorations, and the development or redevelopment of city districts on Greek lines all exemplify the impact of Greek culture in fourth-century Carthage and later. Educated Carthaginians, or many of them, knew Greek; Hannibal himself both spoke it and wrote works in it. By his day the identification of Punic divinities with Greek counterparts was fully developed, as the text of his sworn treaty in 215 with Philip V of Macedon shows.

Carthage was a republic of an individual cast. It practised the only non-Greek political system treated by the philosopher Aristotle around 330 in his work on city-state structures, the *Politics*. (Interestingly, he knew of Rome too, but ignored that city.) It was presided over by two annually elected magistrates called sufetes – Aristotle terms them 'kings' – and by a senate of some hundreds, called The Mighty Ones. The resemblance to Rome's two annual consuls and its senate of some 300 distinguished men is obvious, but two inscriptions of between 500 and 450 BC date themselves to 'the hundred and twentieth year of the sufeteship', which would put its creation near to 600 – almost a century before the consulship. Other Phoenician colonies, too (Gades, for instance), had their own sufetes and senates. The word sufete is much like Hebrew *shophet*, 'judge', and in contrast to Roman consuls they had only civil authority. A council of elders was normal in Mediterranean city-states, and The Mighty Ones held more formal power than their Roman counterparts: if they and the sufetes agreed on a matter – even war and peace – it could be enacted without reference to the citizen assembly. An inner council of thirty, perhaps ex-sufetes, enjoyed specially high status; they may have regulated the agenda for The Mighty Ones and led the way in ceremonial, though little is known of them beyond their eminence.

Lesser magistrates existed as well, as did a number of administrative boards – how chosen, we can only guess – and a high court of 104 whose members were senators appointed by the boards. Separate from all these were the military and naval commands, entrusted to generals elected by the citizen assembly, who might hold their posts for lengthy periods. Adult male Carthaginians formed this assembly, which elected all magistrates and resolved matters brought to it by the sufetes. Still, the limitation, just mentioned, on what it could do made it much weaker than corresponding assemblies in Greece or at Rome. When Polybius claims, disapprovingly, that the citizens of Carthage had the most say in government by 218, this probably meant that the authorities, in practice, were now more inclined to formulate policies which had popular support. That would hardly surprise, for by 218 sufetes and senators were largely members or political allies of Hannibal's family, concerned to maintain high levels of popularity.

It had been Carthage's growing commercial wealth which, during the fifth century, prompted the city to acquire control over the hinterland and its inhabitants. Most of the land in the city's immediate neighbourhood, and the Cape Bon peninsula too, was actual Punic territory, though we do not know how far inland this stretched. Carthage's allies along the coasts – the other Phoenician colonies such as Hippacra and Utica, and cities as far east as Lepcis Magna near modern Tripoli – had territories of their own. The rest of Punic North Africa, roughly northern Tunisia, was the home of Carthage's Libyan subjects in their towns, villages and rural districts. The republic also held the productive lowlands of Sardinia and ports in Corsica, as well as its little island colony of Ebusus (Ibiza) near Spain.

The prosperity of Punic Africa was proverbial. An invading Greek army around 310 was amazed at the rich and readily plundered countryside:

> [it was] divided into gardens and plantations of every kind, since many streams of water were led in small channels and irrigated every part. There were also country houses one after another, constructed in luxurious fashion and covered in stucco ... Part of the land was planted with vines, and part yielded olives and was also planted thickly with other varieties of fruit-bearing trees. On each side herds of cattle and flocks of sheep pastured on the plain, and the neighbouring meadows were filled with grazing horses. ... The leading Carthaginians had laid out there their private estates and with their wealth had beautified them for their enjoyment.[2]

A good deal of this was due to skilful Carthaginian development. A hundred and fifty years later, after sacking Carthage, the Romans took pains to obtain and translate a famous encyclopaedia on agriculture by a Carthaginian writer called Mago. Extracts are found in many Greek and Roman writers on the subject. When Mago lived is not certain but, interestingly, he too was a retired general. Possibly he was Mago 'the Samnite', an old army friend of Hannibal's, taking up his pen after the Second Punic War; but more likely (in view of the already advanced agronomy of the fourth century) he was another Mago well before their time.

Third-century BC Carthage, like Rome, existed in a culturally and politically variegated Mediterranean world. In the east, the conquests of Alexander the Great of Macedon had revolutionised all lands, propagating Greek culture, of varying intensity, and a Greek ruling élite over the ancient kingdoms and states as far as the borders of India. The break-up of his empire had produced three great powers – Macedon, Egypt under the Ptolemies, and the vast realm of the Seleucid dynasty centred around Mesopotamia and Syria – and numerous lesser ones. In the western Mediterranean, only Carthage and Rome were the major states surrounded by smaller neighbours. Some were under their control, like the other Phoenician colonies in Africa and, over in Italy, Rome's autonomous but obedient allies. Others were independent and needing to be carefully handled, like the Numidian peoples to Carthage's west and, until the 220s, the Gauls of north Italy who were neighbours often hostile to the Roman alliance-system.

Carthage and Rome, therefore, were members of a complex and steadily evolving Mediterranean community. It was rare for a state east of the Adriatic and Ionian seas to intervene westwards, though Alexander had supposedly planned to. Pyrrhus of Epirus, a Greek warrior-king with western ambitions, did intervene in Italy and Sicily in the 270s – and failed in both. Reverse intervention had been even rarer: the Romans were the first, imposing a loose hegemony in the 220s over the coastlands of Illyria across the Adriatic. Carthage's interests lay in the central Mediterranean islands and in the far west, especially Spain. But, as the Greek historian Polybius would explain two generations later, it was the war of Hannibal against the Romans that would drive forward the mutual involvement of east and west, and change history.

Hannibal's family

Hannibal's family was of aristocratic blood – royal blood indeed, if we believe that being 'of the Tyrian house of old Barca, he reckoned his ancient forebears from Belus', as the poet Silius claims. Belus had been the father and Barca the loyal brother of Queen Dido; but Silius probably made this up or copied someone who had, for 'Barca' was not a Punic name but a nickname given to Hannibal's father Hamilcar, because of his swiftness in warfare (it seems to mean 'lightning', *baraq*, in Punic), just as 'Barcid' is a modern nickname for the whole family. And 'Belus' looks like a reminiscence of Ba'al, the name of the chief Phoenician and Carthaginian god. If not Silius' own work, the claim probably went back no earlier than when Hamilcar Barca was leader of the state.[3]

The names used by aristocratic Carthaginian men were remarkably few, perhaps a dozen – with Hamilcar, Hannibal, Hanno and Hasdrubal accounting for maybe half of all known Carthaginians – so we cannot tell whether the Barcids were related to any of the earlier leading Hamilcars, Hannibals and Hasdrubals in Carthage's long history. It is quite possible that, instead, they were new on the political scene, ambitious, able and well connected. At all events the family was well-off, perhaps rich. At Carthage, wrote Aristotle in the 330s, wealth was as necessary as good birth for political success, and Hamilcar Barca surely had wealth by inheritance if he

Supposed bust of
Hamilcar (at Rome),
but probably not an
actual portrait.

was 'fairly young' (as Nepos claims) when appointed general in Sicily
in 247. Where the family's affluence first came from, and how they
compared in both aspects with other Carthaginian families, is not
recorded. Merchant trading may well be how Hamilcar's ancestors,
like most of the rest of the city's aristocracy, first rose to affluence,
for the Carthaginians were great sailors and famous as merchants
(not always a reason for praise, in Greek and Roman eyes). All the
same, none of Hamilcar Barca's immediate kin showed affinity

for the sea even if, in later life, Hannibal found himself forced to become briefly a commodore.

Many, if not all, leading families would own estates in Libya, for land was the best investment for well-earned riches. Our only glimpse of Barcid property comes at the moment of Hannibal's exile, when he rode from the city to a 'tower', or castle, of his between the towns of Thapsus and Acholla on the Emporia coast, more than 100 miles away. On the scanty evidence available, the family's status was not primarily – and maybe not at all – due to commercial activity but rather to landed estates, to which they no doubt added substantially with the wealth won by Spanish victories and power.

In 247, whatever Nepos thinks, Hamilcar was thirty or more, for he already had three daughters. His wife is totally unknown, but we can suppose her ancestry too was aristocratic. One of their girls was old enough in 240 to be a prospective wife for a Numidian prince, while another around the same time became wife of Hamilcar's closest political ally, Hasdrubal (called the 'elder' to differentiate him from Hannibal's brother). Again, Hannibal in 218 had a nephew named Hanno son of Bomilcar among his officers: Bomilcar must have been a brother-in-law, and Hanno was surely aged twenty or more in 218, which indicates that his mother (a third sister of Hannibal's) had been born during the 250s at latest.

Hannibal himself entered the family in the second half of 247, the first son for Hamilcar. He was named after his grandfather, a frequent custom at Carthage. Two brothers followed, Hasdrubal ('the younger') in about 244 and Mago around 240. Though Hamilcar was now general in Sicily against the Romans, it is not likely that his wife accompanied him to war and bore two or all three sons in his camps. Hamilcar's camps were more than usually dangerous, on mountain strongholds first near Panormus (Palermo) and then on Mt Eryx (Monte San Giuliano) overlooking Drepana, today's Trápani, with Roman forces harassing them all the time. As well as making naval raids on Italy, therefore, Hamilcar must have visited Carthage at least once and maybe twice. The trip was not too risky, for from 248 until 242 the Romans had no fleet at sea. In spite of his long absences, then, he would not be just a name to his growing family but a lively if maybe awe-inspiring figure.

Hamilcar Barca in the First Punic War

When Hamilcar, still only in his thirties, became general in Sicily, the First Punic War was – astonishingly – in its eighteenth year. Its outbreak in 264 had been preceded by two and a half peaceful centuries of trade and occasional diplomatic relations. Two early treaties defining naval contacts and trade regulations are quoted by Polybius, followed in 279 by a pact of mutual assistance, when both states were confronting Pyrrhus of Epirus (it was never actually invoked). Frustrated in his ambitions, Pyrrhus supposedly foretold that Sicily would become a battle-zone between Carthaginians and Romans.

When the spark did fly, it was over the aid that both states in turn offered to a rogue Sicilian city, Messana – then in the hands of Italian ex-mercenaries called Mamertines – against its more powerful neighbour Syracuse. Perhaps to the surprise of both Carthaginians and Romans, a dispute over this aid before long turned into a conflict between the two foreign powers which soon neutralised the original wranglers, but did indeed make Sicily a quarter-century-long battlefield.

Ancient writers as well as modern differ over why the war came. Explanations include Carthaginian expansionism as a threat to Rome's newly imposed hegemony over south Italy, or Roman expansionism now casting a covetous eye on Sicily and North Africa, or an unscrupulous blend of greed and fear felt by either side towards the other. But, in fact, the Romans first sent forces to support Messana against Syracuse, and until 262 concentrated their efforts in that direction. Greed for Sicilian booty had certainly influenced them. Meanwhile the prospect of Roman hegemony over both Messana and Syracuse – still the chief city-state in Sicily – had almost as certainly appalled the Carthaginians. The spark from a small local war unexpectedly, then, detonated something much vaster. The modern world would experience a similar shock from small origins in July 1914.

Both sides learned much about the other, militarily and psychologically, during the war. The Romans found their first major overseas enemy to be not only a great naval power but also resilient on land, while discovering serious limitations in their own styles of warmaking, especially in leadership and siegecraft. The Carthaginians were staggered when their new foes, traditionally a land power, took to the sea and defeated the veteran Punic navy in battle after battle. Nor were the Romans less resilient after their own defeats, or against storms that too often shattered their unwary fleets. The two sides' stubborn endurance (Polybius compares them to two injured yet indomitable fighting cocks) was quite unlike the Mediterranean world's usual style of war since Alexander the Great. Few such wars lasted more than three or four years, and a couple of defeats usually prompted the loser to seek terms. Even the epic conflict between Carthage and Syracuse fifty years earlier – which at one point saw both a Punic army threatening Syracuse and a Syracusan army under Agathocles threatening Carthage – had ended in 306 after five years.

The quarter-century war wore down both combatants and their allies. The Romans lost only a few battles, including the destruction of their expedition to Africa in 256–255 and a naval defeat outside Drepana in 249, but storms ravaging their fleets cost many more lives. After 248 they virtually gave up naval operations to concentrate on besieging, unprofitably, the Carthaginians' last two strongholds in Sicily: Lilybaeum (modern Marsala) and Drepana. Carthaginian difficulties were revealed in their unsuccessful attempt to borrow the very large sum of 2,000 talents, equal to 12 million Greek drachmas (very roughly, perhaps $US120 million today), from Egypt, and in the unmerciful taxing of their Libyan subjects by a general called Hanno the Great. They skimped on pay for the troops in Sicily, and limited Hamilcar's naval efforts to hit-and-run raids. The Roman authorities, in turn, needed to borrow funds from private citizens to build a new fleet in 242.

Hamilcar as general gave the Romans plenty of trouble, with lightning attacks on their forces in Sicily and raids along the coasts of Italy – thus earning his nickname – but with his limited (and largely unpaid) forces he could try nothing more ambitious. When the Romans put to sea with their new state-of-the-art fleet in 242, Drepana and Lilybaeum were cut off from relief supplies. The war-fleet sent from Carthage, outclassed by its challenger, was shattered on 10 March, 241, off the Aegates Islands near Drepana; and Hamilcar was sent authority to negotiate peace.

CHAPTER 3

BARCIDS SUPREME
(241–221)

The 'Truceless War': Hamilcar saves Carthage

The peace of 241 recognised both the Roman victory and Carthage's endurance. Punic Sicily was given up and a war-indemnity imposed, but no other exactions were forced on the defeated. In recognising each other's territorial integrity and allies, the treaty revealed a wary mutual respect. Even so, the evacuation of Sicily – with a fee imposed by the Romans for every man who came down from Eryx – was humiliating enough to stimulate murmurs and threats against the plenipotentiary general. Hamilcar promptly resigned his command and sailed home, where he found himself sidelined. There was even talk of prosecuting him, though the war had been lost at sea by an admiral whom the high court of 104 had promptly crucified. Rather sketchy evidence in Diodorus and Appian suggests that his popular son-in-law Hasdrubal succeeded in shielding him. And in the meantime Carthage found herself face to face with catastrophe.

It is a cliché that Carthaginians served as crews in the Punic navy, but rarely in the armies – a cliché that applies, in reality, only to the third century when for international wars armies had to be large and professional. Punic armies increasingly consisted of foreign mercenaries and Libyan recruits: the Libyans probably a mix

of conscripts and volunteers, the mercenaries drawn from all over
the Mediterranean. At various times they included Greeks, Gauls,
Spaniards, Campanians from Italy, Ligurians, Balearic slingshot-
throwers, and Numidian cavalry, the best in the western world.
After about 280, war-elephants too began to be used, as they
already were in the Greek East. A Punic army thus formed a very
variegated force, its contingents differing in weaponry, armour
and fighting methods, led by their own officers at unit level who,
in turn, were commanded by senior Carthaginians. Such forces
had enviable advantages: versatility in changing circumstances and
terrains, experience through long service, and the solidarity of old
and trusted comrades. They also had limitations, for men served
Carthage for pay or under compulsion, and alongside men of other
cultures, habits and languages. A long run of defeats or – much
worse – of erratic pay could prompt desertions, betrayals or outright
mutiny. This now happened.

When the republic's undefeated, but long unpaid, veteran
mercenaries and Libyans came back to Africa, they found their
employers anxious to get out of paying the full arrears owed.
Hamilcar had promised them fair treatment, but plainly he and his
friends were no longer powerful enough to ensure it. After much
wrangling with the Punic authorities, the veterans mutinied at
Tunes (today's Tunis) late in 241 and blockaded Carthage itself. The
savage 'Truceless War' would last over three years (to early 237),
be marked by repeated atrocities on both sides, and come near
to destroying the republic. Most of the oppressed Libyans joined
the revolt. With Carthage itself hemmed in and Hanno the Great,
still general in Africa, unable to do more than hold his own in the
countryside, ruin loomed over the city. Before long Hamilcar was
reappointed general as Hanno's colleague.

Hamilcar galvanised operations, combining boldness, guile and
recklessness – and often barely skirting disaster. He broke out of

Carthage to harry the rebel interior, then found himself entrapped between rebel and Numidian forces. At this critical moment a young Numidian prince, Naravas, changed sides, helped him to rout the enemy and became his staunch ally – and, as mentioned above, probably his son-in-law. Later in the war it was the turn of Hamilcar and Naravas to entrap a major rebel army in the countryside, reduce it to cannibalism and then starvation, and induce its leaders to surrender on terms – only to fall on the leaderless rank and file and annihilate them. Later again, when Hamilcar divided his forces to cage the last rebel army in its Tunes camp, this division led to a severe defeat which took months to remedy. Earlier he and Hanno the Great had quarrelled – so badly that their troops had been authorised to choose between them. The men voted to keep him in command and sack his colleague, but the disaster outside Tunes imposed a reconciliation. The two co-ordinated their operations and so at last forced an end to the great rebellion late in 238 or early in 237.

Polybius' account unemotionally, and therefore all the more memorably, conveys the horror and drama of the war – it inspired Gustave Flaubert's graphic novel *Salammbô*. What Polybius leaves implicit but obvious is that all the credit for victory went to Hamilcar. Hamilcar was at once given a fresh command, this time for Spain, leaving behind a political faction which now dominated the republic's affairs. Hanno the Great, despite his eminence, was effectively sidelined from government along with his supporters, to their undying resentment.

Foreign affairs and home politics

During the frenzied struggle for survival, the Carthaginians had not been abandoned by the outside world. Both the prosperous king of Syracuse, Hiero, and the Romans themselves sent supplies and provisions while blocking any to the rebels. The Romans may even have waived a clause in the peace treaty and let Italian mercenaries be recruited for the Punic armies. The shock was all the greater, then, when preparations early in 237 to recover Sardinia (it too had revolted) brought a message from Rome denouncing the preparations as really aimed against Italy, and declaring formal war on the still-shaken republic. The Carthaginians, under Hamilcar's leadership, had to agree to give up all claim to Sardinia and pay over – from what resources we do not know – the huge lump sum of 1,200 talents, or 7.2 million Greek drachmas, to their self-declared adversaries.

This incident was to have profound long-term effects, yet it is not easy to explain why it happened. The Romans had not sought Sardinia previously, and even after seizing it they paid it, like Sicily, only intermittent notice. Moreover they went on to pay the Carthaginians minimal notice too. Roman energies in the 230s and 220s were focused instead on north Italy and across the Adriatic Sea – eventually conquering much of the former and imposing hegemony over the eastern coasts of the latter. Rather than greedy westward imperialism or deliberate provocation, their rape of Sardinia looks like an overreaction to events in North Africa. Hamilcar was the one Carthaginian general they had never defeated. Conceivably, his crushing victory over the rebellion, the move to retake Sardinia, and his evident preparations for a further overseas expedition seemed at Rome a portent that Carthage's ultimate goal was her lost territories in Sicily. The Carthaginians, we may be certain, had no such idea, least of all when much of their own land was in ruins – but military reactions based on inadequate intelligence are not unknown even today.

In reality, the expedition to recover Sardinia would have been a sideshow. The real enterprise was a westward drive into Spain which Hamilcar launched as soon as the crisis was over. It had clearly been planned earlier, for he landed at Gades (Cádiz), another old Phoenician colony, still in the first half of 237. Plainly the expedition was judged essential and urgent. He took his son-in-law Hasdrubal with him as his deputy: a surprise, for Hasdrubal was a popular and political figure at home, not known for military achievements, while Hanno the Great – once the leading man at Carthage – was now their devoted enemy. Yet over the next thirty years and more, Hanno would remain powerless to affect the Barcids' position or policies, while the Carthaginians, on all the available evidence, supported them solidly.

Occasionally in modern scholarship, Hamilcar and then his Barcid successors are portrayed as standing politically for a more democratic Carthage, or as leaders at odds with the established oligarchy and relying on direct consultation of the ordinary citizens. Hasdrubal the elder was certainly popular – though by 237 hardly more so than his father-in-law, the saviour of the republic – and Polybius does remark, unenthusiastically, that the people of Carthage had the chief say in affairs by 218. Yet the Carthaginian senate, on the evidence we have, continued to direct affairs (for instance, accepting war in 218 and making peace in both 203 and 201), while high military and civil offices continued to be held by men of high status. Such men, naturally, had to be either Barcid kinsmen or their political supporters; but this was political reality, not social transformation. Given most Carthaginians' support (as late as 203 or 202) for the Barcids and the war with Rome, Polybius' censorious accusation of democracy looks like a simple exaggeration.

Hannibal's oath

The moment of Hamilcar's departure from Carthage was the setting for the first memorable scene in the life of his eldest son. Polybius records Hannibal describing it forty years later at Ephesus in Asia Minor:

> When my father was about to go on his Iberian expedition I was nine years old: and as he was offering the sacrifice to Zeus I stood near the altar. ... Calling me to him, [he] asked me affectionately whether I wished to go with him on his expedition. Upon my eagerly assenting, and begging with boyish enthusiasm to be allowed to go, he took me by the right hand and led me up to the altar, and bade me lay my hand upon the victim and swear that I would never be friends with Rome.

Roman tradition made subtle changes to this. In Livy's famous account:

> Hannibal, at about the age of nine, was in a boyish fashion trying to coax his father Hamilcar to take him to Spain. Hamilcar ... was offering sacrifice. He brought Hannibal to the altar and there made him touch the sacred objects and swear to make himself an enemy of the Roman people at the earliest possible opportunity.[4]

The Roman version thus makes the child, and necessarily his father, consciously determined to foster enmity between Carthage and Rome. Polybius himself shared this interpretation, and in fact Hannibal told the story to convince Antiochus III, the Great King of the East, that he could be trusted implicitly if the king warred with the Romans. Yet his version of the oath (which Livy supplies later, too) does not automatically imply active enmity. That gives it more credibility than the other, which so much better suits the Romans' view of the Barcids.

The context is important. The Romans had just reversed their friendly attitude and seized Sardinia, declared war on Hamilcar's and Hannibal's homeland on false pretexts, and exacted a second indemnity even larger than the down-payment imposed at the peace in 241. It felt like a stab in the back, the more calculatedly treacherous because the ravaged republic obviously had no option but to acquiesce. Hamilcar, now *de facto* leader of his people and embarking on a grand enterprise to revive their fortunes, cannot have felt anything but disgusted anger at the coup.

The episode made a powerful impression on the boy Hannibal. Polybius' Zeus probably was Carthage's Ba'al Hammon, the greatest of the Punic gods; the ceremony sought the god's favour for the enterprise of Spain and, by extension, for the safety and weal of the republic. Hannibal never forgot it or his oath, even forty years later. It is ironic that Livy, who reports the event twice, also rounds on the Carthaginian for atheism and 'no respect for an oath'.

Hamilcar's new empire in Spain

In Spain Hamilcar meant to build a new Punic province to equal Libya. In the south and east, its peoples lived in small but well-organised communities centred on fortress towns or villages, with a prosperous agriculture and other resources – including precious metals. The ranges north and north-west of the river Baetis (Guadalquivir) stored silver as well as copper; the waters of the river Tagus bore gold dust. Spanish soldiers were hardy, well armed (especially those who used the broad curved sword called the *falcata*) and numerous: good replacements for the Greek mercenaries who no longer seem to figure in Punic armies. All these could be put to the benefit of Carthage.

Carthaginian trade with southern Spain was well established, along with a measure of influence there, as the Punic treaty with Rome in or near 348 shows; stories were told of Carthaginian jealousy and treachery against foreign merchant-interlopers. But direct control was new. The many Phoenician trading ports on the south coasts, such as Gades and Malaca (today's Málaga), had old links with Carthage via her colony on the island of Ebusus (Ibiza) and her little trade-stations along the African coastline. Hamilcar based himself at Gades, and opened a series of campaigns across the south.

Some Spanish communities accepted him and became allies, providing troops and supplies as required. Others had to be forced – and these no doubt had tribute as well as manpower levied from them, under much more authoritarian terms. Hamilcar, already ruthless in the Truceless War, could be just as harsh to Spanish enemies, but he knew when to show mercy as well. Success built on success. In the later 230s he annexed the south-eastern coastlands, only one or two days' sail from Ebusus, and there founded a new city. Its Punic name is unknown; Diodorus calls it by the Greek name Acra Leuce, 'White Fort', and it was in all probability the Lucentum of Roman times, today's Alicante. He now had an urban centre with much shorter communications to Carthage and with room to grow, in contrast to cramped Gades on its small offshore island. By 229 he had created military forces larger than any since the early years of the war with Rome: at least 50,000 infantry and 6,000 cavalry, and a corps of no fewer than 100 elephants.

Hamilcar continued to control affairs in Africa, too. When subject Numidians revolted, Hasdrubal his son-in-law went back to subdue them. The unknown Barcid kinsmen at Carthage, who ensured the continuing political ascendancy of the family and its supporters, performed brilliantly – buttressed, of course, by the stream of victorious wealth that soon began to flow from Spain. We must infer that the sufetes and many or most other magistrates elected yearly were family members, close supporters, or other leading aristocrats who found it wise to ally politically with the Barcids. Over time, too, the membership of the senate and the high court of 104 would embrace more and more such men, although we cannot trace the process in any detail. Hannibal would inherit this successful complex of alliances and patronage.

Meanwhile Hamilcar's province developed well – at least from Carthage's viewpoint. 'With horses, arms, men and money he enriched the whole of Africa,' writes Nepos. Money came not only from taxes and commerce but from mines. The importance of mining is shown, for instance, by the direction of Hamilcar's first operations: against 'Iberians and Tartessians', thus the mining regions around today's Río Tinto north-west of Cádiz, supposed site of the semi-legendary Tartessus (the Bible's Tarshish?). Interestingly, silver coins of Gades in the Barcid period are of a notably higher quality than before. In turn, Hamilcar and his successors struck a fascinating coinage, with profiles of gods whose features (some scholars think) really portray the Barcid leaders themselves. For mining output we have only one reported figure: 300 pounds of silver per day from one mine in Hannibal's day, a rate equivalent to over 100,000 pounds annually – about 1,500 talents or 9 million drachmas; perhaps $US90 million today. This seems exaggerated for a single mine or even mining complex, but might in reality represent all of Punic Spain's annual silver output around 218. Much of this, of course, had to be spent in the province, but revenues of such size vividly illustrate Nepos' assertion about the benefits to Africa.

In his first years in Spain, Hannibal must have spent most of his time at Gades, for it would not be sensible for Hamilcar to take a small boy on campaigns. Hannibal may well have had an older sister to supervise him, for his brother-in-law surely brought his wife to Spain too. Hamilcar of course had to have his son properly educated: thus it was that Hannibal met his Greek tutor Sosylus of Sparta. At some date there arrived, too, Silenus of Sicilian Caleacte. Nepos does not say in what capacity but, as it is not likely that a Sicilian was needed for teaching horsemanship or military arts, we may see him as a literary associate of Sosylus', if not an acquaintance of Hamilcar's from the old days in Sicily. Even in distant Spain the Greek cultural interests of the Barcid circle are evident. Both became friends, companions and lifelong admirers of the young man whose career they were one day to record.

Physical prowess and training in leadership were required too. Just as Hasdrubal was Hamilcar's deputy, Hannibal in turn was readied for major responsibilities. So too were his brothers, the younger Hasdrubal and Mago, who joined him in Spain as they grew older. All three were trained as officers and took part in campaigns over the years. It was probably understood from the beginning that, if anything happened to Hamilcar before he reached old age, their brother-in-law – by 229 a man in his thirties or even forties – would take over the generalship and, with it, primacy in the Barcid faction dominating affairs at home. Then in due time Hasdrubal would be followed by Hannibal. The two seem to have got on well. When Hannibal reached his mid-twenties, he was appointed in effect Hasdrubal's deputy commander. Hamilcar had thus prepared a format for Barcid leadership to continue over decades.

By late 229 both of Hamilcar's older sons were campaigning with him, Hannibal now a vigorous eighteen-year-old. They barely escaped the catastrophe that struck the army and their father in the difficult mountains of the south-west interior. Besieging a fortress town called Helice, Hamilcar as so often before gave way to incaution: as winter came on, he sent most of his forces (elephants included) back to Acra Leuce and welcomed instead a body of new allies from north of the Sierra Morena. These proved treacherous – they attacked and routed his remaining troops, and Hamilcar saved his sons only by separating from them to lead the pursuers away. The path ended on the edge of a furiously flowing river, probably the Tader (modern Segura). In full armour, disdaining capture, Hamilcar urged his horse into the waters and disappeared.

Hasdrubal the elder takes command

Hannibal and his brother made it to Acra Leuce, to be joined by their brother-in-law. The Carthaginians in the army, and then the citizens at home, elected Hasdrubal the elder as the new general. No doubt the brothers joined him in wreaking vengeance on the treacherous Spaniards, the Orissi or Oretanians, the survivors of whom became subjects. Expansion continued; over the next eight years Hasdrubal extended Punic control to the line of the river Tagus and increased the army of Spain to 60,000 foot, 8,000 horse and 200 elephants. Even apart from any troops stationed in Punic Africa, this was a military establishment equal to that of any great power of the eastern Mediterranean, and to the four to six legions, with their Italian allied contingents, put into the field by the Romans for their contemporary wars.

Hasdrubal all the same would leave behind a reputation as a conciliator and consolidator: according to our sources, preferring diplomatic conquests to military ones. Magnificence and charisma, more than ever on the Hellenistic model, marked his leadership. Soon after becoming general, he founded a city of his own on a strategic natural harbour 50 miles south of Acra Leuce, naming it 'Carthage' after his homeland (the Romans, for clarity's sake, called it New Carthage; today it is Cartagena) and built a grand palace on its highest hill. Spaniards and Carthaginians joined in peopling it. From its start the city became the capital of Punic Spain. Its size, splendour and name all advertised the imperial revival of the Carthaginian state under Barcid leadership, and many took notice abroad – including the Romans.

Hasdrubal maintained his father-in-law's methods of government, but with added flair. An early visit to Carthage as general confirmed the family faction's grip over home affairs. Back in Spain he gathered envoys from the many and varied communities now under Punic rule, to have them acclaim him their 'supreme general'. This move suggests that – for propaganda purposes anyway – the peoples of Punic Spain were supposedly in a co-operative alliance under his leadership. He added to this by taking a Spanish wife (Hannibal's sister must have died in the meantime, for Carthaginians were monogamous).

At some date, perhaps now, perhaps a few years later, Hannibal in his turn married a Spanish girl. Very little is known about her. She was from Castulo, an important town just north of the river Baetis, close to today's Linares in a mining region. Silius the epic poet names her Imilce – a Carthaginian name – and claims royal ancestry for her, but this may be about as credible as his pedigree for the Barcids. He also gives them a son, born in 219, whom Hannibal later refuses to hand over to the priests as a child-sacrifice to ensure victory.[5] But the latter item is unbelievable – such child-sacrifice is a purely Silian conceit – and so the son may be a poetic fiction too. Hannibal did not take his wife to Italy (Silius later has her at Carthage), nor does she appear in accounts of his postwar sufeteship and exile; she may have died before then. The marriage may have been a love-match, but it obviously contributed to the Barcids' self-portrayal as patrons and friends, and not merely rulers, of their Spanish peoples. Nor was it novel, since Carthaginian aristocrats (like Hamilcar) had long been happy to form marriage-bonds with Numidian lords, Greek notables and, no doubt, citizens of other Phoenician colonies.

Hannibal and his brothers

The second of Hamilcar's sons, the younger Hasdrubal, had come to Spain before their father's death. During the 220s so did Mago, the third brother. The brothers became practised, energetic and reliable commanders, first as lieutenants to their brother-in-law Hasdrubal and then to Hannibal, later as independent army leaders. During the

220s, if not earlier, Hannibal also formed strong friendships with young Carthaginian officers who would later campaign with him. His best friend, according to Polybius, was another Mago (nicknamed then or later, for unknown reasons, 'the Samnite'). Another friend, also named Hannibal, was nicknamed 'the Gladiator', while by 218 Hanno son of Bomilcar – reportedly Hannibal's nephew, as mentioned above – was a fourth trusted and energetic associate. So was a cavalry officer, Maharbal son of Himilco, who would earn fame later too; and one named Gisco whom we only know from an anecdote at Cannae.

Mago 'the Samnite' and Gisco, described as Hannibal's equals in social rank, came no doubt from families allied with his (perhaps even related to it). By 218 Hannibal may also have had in his entourage two resourceful men of mixed Carthaginian and Syracusan parentage, Hippocrates and Epicydes (unless they joined him in Italy later on). Later too, in 213, we learn of a trusted cavalry officer named Mottones, of Libyan and Phoenician ancestry from Hippacra. We are not told whether Hannibal's trust in him came from long years with the army in Spain, or whether Mottones joined him in Italy perhaps in 215. All the same a modestly detailed picture emerges of a body of reliable, increasingly experienced men – many of them Hannibal's age or younger – who worked with him over many years and were not afraid to offer candid advice when they thought it necessary.

Polybius paints a rather unflattering picture of 'the Samnite' and 'the Gladiator' – and, by association, of their leader and friend. Carthaginians, and also the long-lived Numidian king Masinissa, described Hannibal the Barcid and Mago the Samnite to him as keenly competitive for booty – so competitive that they took care never to serve together in the same military operation, lest they have to share the proceeds. 'The Gladiator' was reputedly a ruthless officer, who at a staff meeting in 218 told his leader that the only way they could make the march to Italy was to train the army to live off human flesh – a suggestion Hannibal rejected. In reality the army would find plenty of provisions even in the Alps; and Hannibal had acquired full information about the region before the expedition started. His friend's comment very likely aimed at underlining the riskiness of the enterprise, rather than making a serious proposition.

As the elder Hasdrubal's closest kinsman, Hannibal would belong to his advisory council and contribute to decision-making. There was much to discuss, within Punic Spain and outside, including a Roman embassy in early 225 – the first diplomatic approach from them in twelve years, and much better-mannered – which negotiated a rather unusual agreement with Hasdrubal. He guaranteed no campaigning north of the river Iberus (the Ebro), and thus reassured them that they would have no extra worries in the west while they coped with a massive invasion of Italy from north Italian and Transalpine Gauls. The *quid pro quo* was practical recognition of Hasdrubal's position as leader of the Carthaginian state, and implicit Roman acceptance of further expansion across most of Spain.

Expansion did continue. In 224 Hannibal, now twenty-three, became his brother-in-law's cavalry commander and, as usual, showed high prowess, winning still more devotion from their long-serving troops. Livy tells a confused tale of him only now being brought over from Carthage to take the post, amid grumblings by Hanno the Great that Hasdrubal was both cementing a Barcid monarchy and lusting after his young kinsman; but this is hostile invention. Hannibal had been in Spain since 237, and sexual innuendo had earlier been directed against his father and brother-in-law.

Three years later, his position unexpectedly changed. Hasdrubal was assassinated by an embittered Spaniard in the second half of 221.

CHAPTER 4

LEADERSHIP AND WAR
(221–216)

Hannibal becomes leader and commander

There was no question who would now take command. Like the murdered Hasdrubal, and like Hamilcar during the war in Africa, Hannibal was acclaimed by the army in Spain (no doubt guided by its Punic officers), then formally elected to the generalship by the citizens at home. His popularity with the troops was enormous and, though Carthage had not seen him since boyhood, he plainly had a high reputation there, too. The Barcid kinsmen and allies who dominated magistracies and senate surely made the succession process run smoothly, for this was in their interest as much as his.

Afterwards, everyone depicted him as coming to power with the fixed agenda of a revenge-war against Rome. The plan (it was, and often is, claimed) had been devised by Hamilcar, furthered by Hasdrubal and launched by Hannibal; the boyhood oath supposedly proved it. Their contemporary, the Roman historian Fabius Pictor, was told that Hasdrubal had tried and failed to make himself king of Carthage, then ruled his province in arrogantly independent style; finally passing it on, along with his own greed and arrogance, to Hannibal, who proceeded to launch the Roman war against the wishes of every person of consequence at home.[6]

The inconsistencies in these claims were glaring, but many people wished to believe them, especially after the war ended in Carthage's defeat. Hannibal's own oath was interpreted as a proof, as we have seen. And when the Carthaginians were forced by Scipio Africanus to seek terms in 203, while Hannibal was still in Italy, their envoys tried to deflect the blame for the war entirely onto him: a negotiating ploy that failed to move Scipio but obviously had more success later with Fabius Pictor. How the second and third Barcid leaders could totally cut free from Carthage, and yet how Hannibal – from Spain – could afterwards drag the republic into a war against the will of its entire leadership, was left unexplained. The fact, too, that the Carthaginians let their navy run down after 237, until when war came there were just 87 ships fit for service against the Romans' known 220 – simple folly if a Roman war was being schemed – was ignored. The Romans themselves had no idea in 218 – still less before – that there was any Barcid war-plan; they made leisurely arrangements to take the initiative against both Spain and Africa, obviously expecting their enemies to be a passive target.

Hannibal himself was to encourage a notion similar to Fabius Pictor's for quite opposite reasons. On being recalled to Africa in 203 to deal with Scipio, he declared (according to Livy):

So Hannibal has not been defeated by the Roman People, ... but by the Carthaginian senate with its carping jealousy. And Publius Scipio will not feel as much delight and exultation over this ignominious departure of mine as will Hanno who, unable to effect it by other means, has crushed our house by bringing down Carthage.[7]

This claim contradicts all the evidence – Livy's included – that Hanno the Great and his circle were political ciphers from 237 until at least 202. Still, it well suited a general who, ending his great enterprise in failure, was predictably anxious to deflect blame from

Supposed bust
of Hannibal
(Naples, Museo
Archeologico).
Strong suspicions
exist that this is a
Renaissance work
rather than an
ancient portrait.

himself. If Hannibal himself did not make the claim in 203 (or even earlier, to his convivial Roman captive Cincius Alimentus), it was one which Silenus and Sosylus would be ready enough to make for him in their histories, whence it too could percolate into Roman narratives. To many, historians and readers alike, it would simply reinforce the ideas that the Barcids had always been at odds with their fellow aristocrats and that the war had been the fruit of long-nurtured dynastic scheming.

Like his predecessors, Hannibal in reality was *de facto* leader of the republic and its empire. They had all been elected to their generalships by the citizens of Carthage; their military competence extended over both Punic Spain and Punic Africa. Again, not only did Hannibal make a propaganda gesture of seeking orders from home in 219, when it came to a showdown with Saguntum, but the Romans' war-ultimatum the following year was sent to Carthage – where it was all but unanimously rejected – and their war-declaration covered Spain as well as Africa. Hannibal's ensuing military arrangements involved not just the Italian expedition but the defence of both Africa and Spain. We hardly need Polybius' emphatic confirmation that the direction of Carthage's strategy, throughout the war, rested with him:

> It is notorious that he managed the Italian campaigns in person, and the Spanish by the agency of the elder of his brothers, Hasdrubal, and subsequently by that of Mago ... Again, he conducted the Sicilian campaign at first through Hippocrates and afterwards through Mottones the Libyan. So also in Greece and Illyria.[8]

Coming to power at twenty-six, and having left his homeland sixteen years before, Hannibal must have relied on already prominent Barcid kinsmen and allies to maintain family dominance there. Bomilcar his brother-in-law, who held the sufeteship at least once, seems one such, and so too a 'close Barcid relative' named Mago (a cousin?), who became a Roman prisoner in Sardinia some years later. We can reasonably suppose that there were other relatives in public life as well. The fathers and kinsmen of trusted officers such as Mago the Samnite and Hannibal the Gladiator were surely close to the Barcids and politically important. Rising to prominence around this time, too, was another man of high social rank and influence: Hasdrubal son of Gisco. He was to become, for a time, the leading man at Carthage in Hannibal's absence and yet, on the evidence, remained a vigorous ally till his death. It is not too daring to see him as a supportive, but independent, leader of his own group of kinsmen and supporters.

A new leader had to prove his worth right away; so late in 221 Hannibal subdued the Olcades, a Spanish people who probably held lands in central eastern Spain. This may have been unfinished business of his brother-in-law's, but in the next year Hannibal struck far into the north-west against the Vaccaei, dwellers in and cultivators of the plains around the river Durius (Duero). Their towns Helmantica (modern Salamanca) and Arbocala were stormed, the latter with some difficulty, and plenty of booty and captives won. These successes were followed by a victory on the banks of the Tagus against the warlike Carpetani (the people of Old Castile's plateau and mountains) and their allies, including Olcades exiles, who had combined to waylay him on his return march. Hannibal manoeuvred deftly, crossing the river southwards but then waiting on his pursuers, who were attacked and shattered when their forces divided for their own crossing.

There had been no *casus belli* against the Vaccaei, but military glory and plunder were essential to the charisma of a new Barcid chief. A broader result, which Hannibal may have sought too, was to overawe the greater part of Spain between the Tagus and the Ebro into accepting Punic hegemony. One place that did, perhaps more willingly than most, was the small town of Turis, on the east coast where a river, still called the Turia, enters the Mediterranean at Valencia. It was the enemy of a richer and stronger neighbour not far to the north, the city-state of Saguntum (Sagunto today). With the Saguntines firmly against offering similar submission, the Turitani very possibly reckoned on having powerful new support – Hannibal's – in their quarrel. The consequences were more momentous than they can have imagined.

The clash with Rome over Saguntum

The Saguntines had a notional friendship with Rome, perhaps originally from trade, which they took a good deal more seriously than the Romans did. Their regular messages about Punic doings in Spain left the Romans uninterested – until Hannibal extended Carthage's sway, however light in practice, to the Ebro. This brought Roman attention back to Spain after half a decade of ignoring it. In autumn 220 a two-man embassy was sent over, to urge him to respect the Ebro-line and not to trouble the Saguntines. Somewhat earlier, perhaps through the same envoys, the Romans had intervened at the town to settle internal political dissension, using the rough method of putting to death one side's leaders. Hannibal found the envoys waiting at New Carthage when he returned to winter there.

The Romans' motives were probably to size up Carthage's new young leader (this was their first contact with him), remind him of his obligations – though in fact the Ebro agreement had been struck only with Hasdrubal – and, rather incidentally, safeguard the Saguntines in case he was thinking of backing their neighbours. Hannibal responded with anger, but limited himself to accusing the Romans of mistreating the Saguntines in their recent intervention, and to signalling that he would counter-intervene in his turn. As soon as the envoys had gone, he arranged for formal, and evidently public, authorisation from home to do exactly that; and when spring 219 came he put Saguntum under siege. It took a long and arduous seven and a half months, but late in the year he took and sacked the town.

These events became unhelpfully confused in later accounts. The Romans of 219 perplexed their descendants by totally ignoring the beleaguered town – in fact they sent both consuls off in the opposite direction, to fight a new Illyrian war – and so later tradition claimed that the siege occurred in 218 and the embassy was sent then, to try to stop it. Only Polybius dates the mission to 220, but his report is plainly more coherent. Hannibal's anger may have been calculated: he did not threaten the Romans but publicly signalled that he would accept no interference in Spain (and Saguntum, after all, lay far south of the Ebro). At the same time, he fully realised that the Romans might treat an attack on Saguntum, so soon after their warning, as a *casus belli*. He surely suspected them of looking for a way to raise mischief in Punic Spain. In any case, he was not minded to put an end to Spanish campaigning, aged only twenty-seven and commanding large and seasoned forces. Fresh campaigns, in turn, would need to be fought north of the Ebro: another thing likely to annoy the Romans.

After sacking Saguntum, he made suitable preparations. Much of the town's plunder went to Carthage to firm up political support: this was all the more necessary if the Romans did take matters further. Messengers were sent to north Italy to sound out its recently subdued and very discontented Gauls. Meanwhile Hannibal brought troops over from Africa in exchange for Spanish units despatched there, as a way of interlinking the military defence of both lands. His other forces, much larger even than Hasdrubal's yet full of veterans, were rewarded and rested, while he and Carthage waited on events.

The Romans surely had not meant to provoke a war; only to make clear to the new leader his obligations to avoid causing them worry while they pursued interests elsewhere. The Punic republic, defeated in war and taught a further lesson over Sardinia, would be allowed to act as it chose – so long as it respected that limitation. Hannibal's calculated defiance left them in a quandary. Saguntum was not sent help. Instead there were indecisive debates over how to react. Only when winter news arrived of the sack was it decided to make this an issue. At the start of spring 218 a five-man embassy sailed to Carthage to call for the surrender of Hannibal and his advisers for punishment. It was all a performance for public consumption: as they had shown with Hasdrubal, the Romans knew where power really lay in the republic. Naturally the sufetes and senate rejected their demand, the chief Roman envoy announced war with a theatrical shake of his toga, and the Carthaginians shouted their assent.

The invasion plan

The Second Punic War thus opened. Our sources see it as Hannibal's doing: the fulfilment of the Barcid plan for revenge. Moderns are divided, mostly between those who agree with the ancient diagnosis and others who ascribe it to Roman greed for the riches of Spain, anxiety over the resurgence of Carthage's power, or a blend of both. In fact, it looks like an unplanned collision of two wary and prickly states, each sensitive to questions of face and status, both of them assertive and long conditioned to seeing military action as a solution to difficult power relationships. Since each side expected decisive victory and believed (as we shall see) that it knew the other's weaknesses, war looked a better option than years of uneasily risky coexistence.

Hannibal's actions show that he had a rational plan for victory. Unlike the Carthaginians in the previous war, but like Alexander against Persia, he would strike directly at the enemy's heartland. As he lacked a viable fleet, he would strike by land, over the Alps. This offered the extra advantage of bringing him into the midst of the already rebelling north Italian Gauls, so that by adding them to his own troops he could lead an overwhelming invasion force into enemy territory. He was confident of winning the battles that would follow, and to win them so massively that the non-Roman Italians, from Etruria to Bruttium, would be eager to join him and free themselves from Roman hegemony. A shattered, shrunken Rome, bereft of allies, would have no choice but to seek the terms that he would dictate. Hamilcar's humiliation at Mount Eryx would be reversed. More important, Carthage under Barcid leadership would win undisputed hegemony over the western Mediterranean world. Rome would not be destroyed, but would play a suitably diminished rôle in the new system.

Everything hinged on a successful march to Italy. Yet the war's first stage was leisurely. On news of the declaration of war, Hannibal first reviewed his troops at New Carthage, then sent them on furlough, while he himself (and perhaps his brothers Hasdrubal and Mago) journeyed to make sacrifices and offer vows to Melqart at Gades. Then they all reassembled at the capital, where he appointed Hasdrubal as his replacement in Spain. His younger brother, his friends Hannibal the Gladiator and Mago the Samnite, Hanno his nephew, and the cavalry commander Maharbal remained with him. Now at last he led out the expeditionary army northwards. Still his lack of hurry continued, with weeks spent fighting in northern Spain, then a not very pressured march to the Rhône – about 200 miles in three to four weeks. It looks deliberate.

The Romans planned attacks on both Spain and Africa, but took their time over both. There was at least one Punic agent at Rome, not caught until 216, who could have fed information out to Spain or Carthage. If Hannibal could corner the consul Scipio, heading for Spain, and destroy him, it would make the invasion of Italy easier and might spark panic there. A powerful opening blow was needed for another reason too. The other consul, Longus, was preparing an invasion of Africa, where – Hannibal well knew – Carthage had no commander of note. He had to intimidate the enemy, therefore, into calling Longus back.

If Polybius is right that the march to Italy took five and a half months, and the army reached the final crest of the pass 'close to the setting of the Pleiades' (late October or early November), then the men left New Carthage sometime during May. So late a date seems impossible to many, who treat 'the setting of the Pleiades' as merely a fuzzy reference to the approach of winter, and so date the march from early April to late September. So sweeping a reinterpretation of Polybius' one firm date-indicator, which Livy echoes and no other source contradicts, is perilous and unnecessary. Even an early November arrival allows enough time for the recorded campaign events down to the battle of the Trebia, around 22 December.

The march across the Alps

The march to Italy is the single most famous episode in Hannibal's long career. Drama and myth began to cluster around it from early on. Hannibal himself contributed to these for, according to his friend and biographer Silenus, on the march to the Ebro he dreamed that Zeus (thus probably Ba'al Hammon) gave him a divine guide for the expedition:

> the guide instructed him not to look behind. But ... overcome with desire, he did look behind; then he saw a huge and monstrous beast, entwined with snakes, wrecking all trees, thickets and buildings wherever it advanced ... The god answered that it was the ravaging of Italy and instructed him to hasten onwards, not to concern himself with what was happening behind.[9]

This dream may not have been just an invention (though if it was, its form is equally striking). For him and his Carthaginians, the expedition was blessed by heaven and promised to bring disaster on the Romans. The resemblance to the myth of Orpheus and Eurydice, but this time with a favourable outcome, is another token of the Barcids' attachment to Greek culture and Hannibal's own confidence.

The size of his forces has been debated since his own time. Polybius' 90,000 infantry and 12,000 cavalry are widely doubted, though they seem to be Hannibal's figures in an inscription he set up much later at Cape Lacinium (Capo Colonna) in Italy. Polybius interpreted them as the expedition's strength alone, but more likely they include the 15,000 troops left with his brother Hasdrubal. Subduing Spain's north-east then cost heavy casualties, and a strong force of 11,000 was assigned to garrison the region – while ten thousand Spanish mercenaries, unwilling to cross the Pyrenees, went home. Such reductions could account for Hannibal entering southern Gaul with only the 50,000 foot and 9,000 horse that Polybius reports. Overall the Carthaginians' land forces, including those left in Spain and those in Africa, totalled over 120,000 at the outset of war – far more than the 71,000 levied by the Romans, whose sources of information about their enemies were clearly inferior in many areas.

War-making can, all the same, inflict surprises on even the best-prepared plans. At the river Rhône, only a few weeks after the Pyrenees, army numbers were down to only 38,000 foot and 8,000 horse – this before any battles outside Spain had been fought. One suggestion is that Hannibal was leaving garrisons at various strong-points en route, but that is backed by no evidence. Another view is that Polybius' figures for the Rhône crossing are mere exaggerations; but Hannibal was to reach Italy with even fewer troops. Most probably, desertions occurred as the Spaniards and Libyans confronted the prospect of campaigning in a distant land full of powerful foes – and of having to penetrate terrifying mountains first. This problem would only worsen in coming weeks.

The consul Scipio finally embarked for Spain only as Hannibal was crossing southern Gaul, for the marching Carthaginians and Scipio's transport fleet reached the Rhône area at more or less the same time. Now Hannibal decided to avoid confrontation. Even if victorious, he could not then reach Italy before the depths of winter or even (if the passes were snowed in) before spring 217. Instead, sweeping aside the Gauls who sought to stop him crossing, he swung north. Friendlier Gauls helped the footsore army with supplies and escorted it part of the way towards the greatest hurdle of all, the Alps. Scipio, frustrated, made a major strategic decision: he sent his troops on to Spain under his older brother's command, while he himself turned back for north Italy and the legions there.

The epic of Hannibal climaxes in popular memory with the crossing of the Alps, leading an army of infantry, cavalry and their horses, thousands of pack-animals, and the corps of elephants. The entire crossing took only fifteen days, but these were certainly the most dramatic in their participants' lives. Despite all his careful earlier diplomacy, one Gallic people after another proved hostile: the wealthy (to them) and vulnerably extended marching columns represented the loot of a lifetime. Repeated defensive battles up and down the line had to be fought, at heavy loss – at one point, he and the infantry were cut off overnight from the cavalry and pack-animals; sometimes only the terrifying presence of the elephants repelled the Gauls. When the attacks ceased and the expedition crested the final pass, then came an equally painful descent. Polybius describes it:

> the path down was narrow and precipitous, and the snow made it impossible for the men to see where they were treading, while to step aside from the path, or to stumble, meant being hurled down the precipices. ... [Where the road narrowed from a recent landslip, and a fresh snowfall lay atop old ice], the men found both their feet slipping from under them, as though they were on hard ground with a layer of mud on the top. ... Not being able to get a foothold on the lower snow, when they fell and tried to get themselves up by their hands and knees, the men

found themselves plunging downwards quicker and quicker, along with everything they laid hold of.

It took three days' work to rebuild the road at the landslip, and it was here, Livy famously reports, that the men poured vinegar over superheated rock to soften it for splitting (a solution that his contemporary, the architect Vitruvius, attests for lava-rocks at least). Only after a further three-day descent did the weary army come down to the north Italian plains.[10]

The route over the Alps is the most discussed, and disputed, topic in the Hannibalic canon. In spite of seemingly helpful details, like Livy mentioning a crossing of the river Durance and the famous scene of Hannibal at the top of the pass pointing out the plains of Italy to his weary troops, the question turns essentially on how to interpret his and Polybius' accounts – issues, that is, of textual arrangement and literary style. No pass seems to offer both room for a large army and also a view of the plains (the view may be a literary embellishment). Polybius mentions as few geographical names as he can; Livy contradicts or misunderstands some of Polybius' details, and his Durance is described in terms of that river's lower reaches even though his own account implies the upper ones. What really matters is that the army debouched into the lands of the unfriendly Taurini around modern Turin, crushed them, and then took stock.

Hannibal's roll-call revealed, he wrote later, only 20,000 infantry and 6,000 cavalry. The numbers that had crossed the Rhône had been almost halved; of those who had crossed the Pyrenees some ten weeks earlier, little more than two in five were left. Suggestions that his memoir artfully left out as many as 8,000 light-armed troops, who then turn up at the battle of the Trebia, fail to convince; for he was soon joined by thousands of enthusiastic north Italian Gauls (including 4,000 horse) and yet had only 40,000 men, horse and foot, at the battle. Many of the Trebia's 8,000 light-armed must, in fact, have been Gauls, and the rest been part of his own 20,000 infantry. Some of the losses since the Rhône may well have occurred when the army came to rest on the plains – desertions again – but it was a near-disastrous diminution of the grand army that he had so carefully created.

The first battles: Ticinus and Trebia

None the less, Africa was saved. The consul Longus was recalled to bring his forces north. The invasion rolled on; in a cavalry clash by the river Ticinus, the Roman squadrons were beaten and Scipio himself badly wounded – saved by the bravery, it was said, of his seventeen-year-old son and namesake, who would make his own impact on history later. When the energetic Longus arrived with his legions and took over effective command, Hannibal soon induced him to engage the invaders on a broad plain beside the river Trebia, near Placentia (Piacenza), on 22 or 23 December 218.

It opened as a standard ancient battle, one army in regular array moving up to fight the other – but only after he had enticed the enemy to wade at dawn to his side across the ice-cold Trebia. Then Hannibalic variations came into play. First, his superior cavalry, and the elephants, routed the Roman horse, but instead of pursuing these into the distance (a common cavalry habit) his riders re-formed to assault the Roman infantry's now unprotected flanks. Next, his brother Mago with 2,000 picked men climbed out of a deep watercourse that lay unnoticed behind the legions, and charged into their rear. Even though 10,000 Roman infantry burst right through the opposing lines and got away, along with most of the Roman cavalry, three-quarters of the army was slaughtered or taken prisoner. Hannibal's losses were small, and mainly Gallic.

His first full-scale clash with a Roman army illuminates many of his tactical principles. The essential start was to draw the enemy

Etruscan painted dish in the Museo Etrusco di Villa Giulia, Rome. The accompanying baby elephant adds a whimsical touch. Reproduced with kind permission of the Museo Etrusco.

onto terrain that Hannibal chose, at a time that he chose – a difficult art, but helped by the enemy's eagerness to fight. The next stage was to offer what looked like the standard battle format – infantry against infantry, cavalry versus cavalry – but to arrange a stroke that would take the enemy by surprise. In actual combat he used cavalry more resourcefully than any general since Alexander, a flexibility feasible only with disciplined horsemen under reliable commanders. Vigorous pursuit was the final essential to a victory, another Alexander trait.

For these tactics he had to keep his men in good spirits, well equipped and supplied, and intelligently led – not only by himself but by skilful and inspiring officers. Of these at the outset of the war he had plenty: his brother Mago and nephew Hanno, a Hasdrubal who was to perform brilliantly at Cannae, and Maharbal and Carthalo (two more cavalrymen), not to mention his friends 'the Samnite' and 'the Gladiator'. His war council must have comprised the ablest group of officers since Alexander's – or one even abler. Care of his men was crucial too. He devoted care and time to foraging, capturing enemy supply depots, and looking after his wounded and the all-essential horses.

The whole of north Italy, save for a few Roman-held towns, was now in his hands and so was the strategic initiative. Hoping to build on it, he sent home all his non-Roman Italian prisoners without ransom, with the message that he had come to free Italy from its Roman masters. He surely did not expect immediate responses; but the propaganda would be backed up by his next move, southwards into the Italian peninsula. That move, though, had to wait until spring. A bitter winter closed down all operations and, worse, killed many of the troops and all but one of the surviving elephants. It also caused some discontent among the newly acquired Gallic allies – unwilling to march south, perhaps. Then, as soon as weather permitted, he struck across the Appenines into Etruria.

At this point the plan may have been to strike directly at Rome. For, some time later, in summer, a fleet from Carthage arrived off the coast at Pisae (modern Pisa), 'expecting to join up with Hannibal here'.[11] This must have been prearranged – and well in advance, for he had had no means of contacting Carthage after leaving Spain – and the only reason for a war-fleet meeting him on the coast of Etruria would be for a joint operation southwards.

If so, he had intended this move at the start of the expedition. But the first news the Carthaginians were to get from him were despatches sent from the Adriatic coast after Trasimene; obviously these showed that his plans had changed. By then, though, the fleet had sailed for Italy.

The battle of Lake Trasimene

For 217 the Romans elected as one consul a vigorous and experienced leader, Flaminius, who had played a major part in the conquest of north Italy in the 220s. His combativeness would be to Hannibal's advantage. Meanwhile more difficulties dogged the invaders: the spring floods turned the middle reaches of the river Arno into deep marshlands, and a four-day march through them into a nightmare.

> Everything was covered with water, and finding a dry spot to set down their wearied limbs was impossible. And so they would pile their baggage packs together in the water and lie down on them; or the cadavers of pack animals that were strewn in heaps all along their path provided as much of a bed as they needed. All they sought was something above water that would give them a moment's sleep.[12]

Hannibal himself, riding on the one surviving elephant and already suffering from an attack of ophthalmia, emerged from the Arno marshes virtually blind in his right eye. Now he faced the threat of two consular armies – that of Flaminius to his left at Arretium (Arezzo) in central Etruria, that of Servilius at his rear at Ariminum (Rimini) on the Adriatic.

Yet it proved a simple matter to lure Flaminius to the right spot. By first ravaging the countryside, then turning left to pass Lake Trasimene, Hannibal seemed to asking for entrapment between the two consuls. In furious pursuit, marching in column without forward scouting, Flaminius with his two legions reached the northern shores of the lake in the mist-laden dawn of 21 June, and were struck all along their strung-out left flank by the Punic army in ambush on the hillsides.

The Romans were unable to form up, their officers unsure what was happening, Flaminius helpless to exert control. Even so it took three hours to destroy the legions. The victory was still more shattering than at the Trebia – the consul and 15,000 men killed or drowned, another 15,000 taken, barely 1,500 Punic losses (mainly Gauls again). The tireless Maharbal, fresh from capturing the only organised body of enemy troops to break free, then smashed 4,000 cavalry that Servilius had sent ahead to reinforce Flaminius. With no cavalry and his two legions heavily outnumbered, Servilius dared not move further. Nothing except some surviving fugitives stood between Hannibal and Rome, four days' march to the south. Terror and dread reigned in the city, cut off from Servilius and, at best, with only two legions of raw recruits within the walls. There were troops at Tarentum (Taranto) and in Sicily, but effectively these were out of contention too.

Again Hannibal set free his non-Roman captives with his message of freedom for Italy. He also tried, unsuccessfully, to find and bury Flaminius' body. He now made perhaps his most important decision of the war. The Punic fleet would not find him on the Tuscan coast: 'feeling now entirely confident of success,' Polybius writes, 'Hannibal rejected the idea of approaching Rome for the present; but traversed the country plundering it without resistance, and directing his march towards the coast of the Adriatic.'[13] The ferocious stubbornness of the legions, even in catastrophe, perhaps turned him against assaulting their city. He may have reckoned, instead, that to capitalise on Trasimene by advancing into the midst of the peninsula's allied states would galvanise them into defection. Besides, his own troops and horses were in poor condition despite

An infantryman's mailcoat, reconstructed from remnants found in Lake Trasimene. Possibly or probably of third-century BC date, and possibly the armour of a drowned Roman or allied Italian soldier. Reproduced from *The Armour of Imperial Rome* by H. Russell Robinson (London: Arms and Armour Press, 1975).

the victory, making a march into unspoiled, well-stocked territories advisable.

It was a surprising decision all the same, for Etruria and the regions around Rome were hardly less productive or, in midsummer, less well provisioned. Indeed, some if not all of his officers may have expected just such a move. The famous story of cavalryman Maharbal, offering to ready him a feast on Rome's Capitoline hill 'on the fifth day' after battle if the cavalry were sent ahead, is placed by our sources on the day following Cannae. In fact they may go back to an account (Coelius', perhaps), which displaced it from Trasimene – a battlefield 85 miles, four days' march, from Rome, not 300 miles like Cannae. The advance of the army, with its roaming patrols of Numidian, Spanish and Gallic horsemen, could have obstructed – or even disrupted – the Romans' frantic levying of fresh troops, and worsened the panic inside the city; and, especially if the fleet from Carthage were in support, could have cut off all supplies from outside. Storming Rome would not have been necessary. Yet the impression made on her already shocked allies would have been staggering.

Hannibal versus Fabius the Delayer

Hannibal rearmed his Libyan infantry with the plentiful high-quality Roman weaponry taken from the enemy dead and prisoners, then turned eastwards to refresh his army in the coastlands of the Adriatic and send a victory despatch homeward by sea. Next he marched south into Apulia, a good 300 miles from Lake Trasimene. Now high summer had come, with plenty of food in the fields and barns. At the same time he had also given the Romans time to regroup.

The emergency office of dictator, with supreme military command, was conferred on Quintus Fabius Maximus, an eminent senator who had twice been consul, with another ex-consul, Minucius, as his master of horse or deputy. Four more legions were in the field, and Fabius brought an entirely different approach to operations – one not only disagreeable to the Carthaginians, but hardly less so to his fellow citizens. Fabius was elderly, had last commanded an army a decade and a half earlier, and preferred caution to panache. His family, interestingly, had Carthaginian connections: Carthalo, one of Hannibal's staff-officers, was a hereditary guest-friend.

Hannibal found the dictator constantly refusing battle. Instead his army was shadowed by the Romans moving along nearby hills, harassing his columns, and cutting off strays and foragers as he marched westwards out of Apulia, through the mountains of Samnium and into Campania. Eventually this almost brought a disaster: for even though the dictator's 'Fabian tactics' infuriated his own citizens, they revealed important limitations in both Hannibal's army and his grand design. The army was invincible on more or less level ground but, like most regular armies – and their generals – was incapable of operating aggressively in hill or mountain country. Attacking or entrapping Fabius in his own positions was thus out of the question. Yet an enemy who accepted looting and destruction, in return for attritional warfare without battle, effectively held the better hand. With no firm bases, no Italian defections, and no steady contact with home or Spain or replenishments from either, Hannibal and his men were wanderers – destructive wanderers, but at risk of withering away without a prospect of ultimate victory.

One reason for entering Campania was that a trio of Campanian aristocrats captured at Trasimene had agreed to try to win over for him its chief city, Capua (Santa Maria Capua-Vetere). This failed to happen, so the army contented itself with looting and burning the rich countryside north of the river Volturnus, while Fabius' legions observed them from the heights to the east. Hannibal tried a little psychological warfare, ostentatiously sparing a local estate of the dictator's (a stratagem once practised by the Spartans against Pericles) in hopes of prompting suspicions of some secret link between them. Nevertheless he had decided to return to Apulia. The decision remains something of a surprise, for Campania – or a height like the broad Mt Tifata, overlooking Capua, which he indeed used later – would have offered a relatively safe and stockable base, as well as more direct communication with Carthage and more encouragement to friendly elements at Capua and other towns. The risk of trouble from the Romans was about the same in either region. In fact, Fabius' dictatorship, already under heavy criticism even from his master of horse, had a strict six-month limit and Hannibal could hope for the next commander or commanders to be more aggressive (as indeed they were). A pitched battle on the Campanian plains, rather than Apulia's, would have been at least as decisive and maybe more so. Instead, by deciding to leave, and via the same pass north of Teanum (Teano), he almost walked into Fabius' grasp.

The dictator had blocked the pass through the hills and placed troops on both sides. With his army slowed by plundered goods and animals, Hannibal could not risk trying another exit and meeting another barrier. He turned Fabius' caution to his own profit. Ordering bundles of dry faggots to be tied to the horns of the biggest oxen and then set afire, he had the unhappy animals driven forward during the night to a hill nearby, and so drew off the alarmed enemy troops holding the pass. Fabius, cautious literally to a fault, did nothing lest he fall into a night trap. Hannibal marched coolly away – also, with his usual care, rescuing the soldiers detailed to handle the oxen. Not only did he return to Apulia but his humiliation of Fabius strengthened the combative Minucius' arguments for a fresh offensive. In further foraging around the captured town of Gereonium, between Luceria and Larinum (Lucera and Larino), a small victory by the master of horse then allowed Hannibal to entice his half of the army into a trap, again one involving Punic troops hidden in gullies on a seemingly level plain. Not perhaps not to Hannibal's great surprise, Fabius arrived at the last moment with the other legions to stop the trap from closing. With winter drawing near, operations then fizzled out. More remarkably, they remained on hold until midsummer 216.

The Romans had decided to create the largest army in their history to crush Hannibal by main force. Instead of four legions of Romans and Italian allies facing him, they would put eight into the field, equip and train them thoroughly, and then bring him to pitched battle. The great army, vast enough to outnumber him overwhelmingly, would make ambushes or traps futile. Paradoxically, this required the troops in Apulia, now under interim commanders, to continue Fabian tactics after Fabius stepped down. Even more paradoxically, it put Hannibal and his army into difficulties. He had 50,000 troops, 10,000 of them cavalry, for whom the supplies gathered in Campania and Apulia would hardly suffice for months on end. Over the winter and spring, with little foraging available and no more towns or depots taken, rations – especially for the horses – must have become steadily tighter. Livy reports complaints, unrest and even desertion threats growing as 216 wore on, reports that are not provable fictions.

Even worse, politically and diplomatically the invasion was deadlocked. If the enemy continued merely dogging Hannibal's forces, hampering his supplies, and harassing his movements without standing to battle, it made a spectacle that would scarcely attract even the most restive Italians. News from Spain, if it trickled through, was not good either: in 217 his brother Hasdrubal was badly beaten by the Roman invaders under the brothers Publius and Gnaeus Scipio, who began to make inroads into Punic territory (Publius as consul in 218 had been assigned Spain). The Romans were expanding their land and sea forces alarmingly too: besides the legions coming up to face him, another eight were on service in north Italy, Sicily and Spain, while the Roman navy remained at full strength. The Punic navy was growing, but (perhaps wisely) it avoided combat. The Barcids' dominance in the republic at home depended vitally on military success, and this had come to a standstill.

Cannae: The crowning victory?

It is likely enough that Hannibal surmised a change was coming. Whether or not his spy at Rome passed on word, the levying and preparation of the super-army during the first months of 216 could hardly be kept secret, with recruits and armaments being drawn from all over Italy. Once the harvest was in, he forced the pace, shifting to Cannae further south where he took a well-stocked depot on a hill overlooking a broad, unbroken plain. The new consuls, Aemilius Paullus and Terentius Varro, had to follow: the Senate had ordered battle. On 2 August, with Varro holding that day's command, they offered it near Cannae beside the river Aufidus.

Hannibal's forces were facing some 70,000 Roman and Italian foot and 6,000 horse; another 10,000 held the two Roman camps nearby. Seasoned though his men were, the size of the enemy army was troubling. As Hannibal and his senior officers surveyed it from a hillock,

> Gisco, a Carthaginian of equal rank with himself, told him that the numbers of the enemy were astonishing; to which Hannibal replied with a serious countenance, 'There is one thing, Gisco, yet more astonishing, which you take no notice of'; and when Gisco inquired what, answered, that 'In all those great numbers before us, there is not one man called Gisco.'[14]

It was the right joke for the situation. The entire company broke into laughter and the laughter spread through the ranks. The Carthaginians then proceeded to destroy the Roman super-army.

Many details in the battle of Cannae are debated, including which side of the Aufidus it was fought on (and what the river's course was in 216), as well as how or if to reconcile conflicting tactical items in the sources. Still, the crucial features are clear. With cavalry positioned on the wings of both armies, and the Aufidus as extra protection for the Roman right, the legions and Italian allies massed in dense lines – rather than the usual chessboard formation of legionary companies – to bear down on the Punic centre like a juggernaut. The consuls would recall how some of the Roman centre had smashed a way through at the Trebia; they surely reckoned that now, with twice as many infantry as Hannibal's, not just a breakthrough but a rout would follow. That this would be their tactic was obvious from the legions' array, nor in any case were Roman infantry trained for much manoeuvring save frontal attack. Hannibal stationed Gallic and Spanish soldiers in his front, forming a shallow line with only the usual light-armed skirmishers ahead of them. Then, instead of a parallel line of his remaining infantry behind, he drew up the now Roman-equipped Libyan infantry in two columns, one behind either end of the front line. A broad expanse of empty ground was left between the columns, while Maharbal perhaps held the rear with a small cavalry reserve.

Only an army of unrivalled experience, under officers solidly reliable and unusually intelligent, could manoeuvre this brittle-looking array into a stupendous victory. As the legions pressed forward, the Gauls and Spaniards gave ground, at first without breaking. The Roman infantry crowded forward into the empty ground between the Libyan columns. The advancing troops must now have seen these through the dust-clouds but, caught in the momentum of the advance, could do nothing about them. They must have hoped that the Roman and allied cavalry would be able to distract them. The cavalry, however, was out of the fray. Beside the Aufidus, the Roman citizen horse had been driven back by the Spanish and Gallic cavalry under an officer named Hasdrubal, while on the opposite wing the Italian allied squadrons grappled with Hannibal's Numidians. In a brilliant move, Hasdrubal took several of his Spanish and Gallic units right around behind the legions to fall on the rear of the Italians, who broke in turn.

About this time, Hannibal's stretched and harried front line finally ruptured. Hannibal, unusually, entered the fight himself to rally them – perhaps he brought in Maharbal's cavalry reserve. Now the Libyan columns turned about, formed line along the flanks of the legions and charged. Crowded together, jostling for room, the legionaries on the flanks struggled in groups or individually to face the new assault. The entire Roman infantry mass started to lose cohesion. At this point Hasdrubal, leaving the Numidians to chase the enemy horse into the distance, regrouped his Spanish and Gallic squadrons yet again, to launch attacks on the enemy infantry from the rear.

The slaughter that followed dwarfed that of the British army on the first day of the Somme, twenty-one centuries later. On Livy's figures (for once less sweeping, and more credible, than those of Polybius) over 50,000 Romans and Italians, mostly infantry, were dead by nightfall. Among them were the consul Aemilius Paullus, Minucius the former master of horse, and Servilius the previous year's other consul, along with twenty-nine of the legions' forty-eight senior officers (military tribunes) and eighty senators or senatorial candidates. The garrisons in the main Roman camp and a subsidiary one nearby surrendered; in all nearly 20,000 prisoners were taken. The surviving consul, Varro, strenuously rallied all the survivors he could (and was thanked by the Senate 'for not having despaired of the state'): they amounted to a slim 14,500. The rest of the super-army had been annihilated.

Hannibal's dead were around eleven per cent of his troops, chiefly Gauls again, a significant proportion of his army. His compensation was a victory that at last split open the Romans' system of alliances and made Carthage the pre-eminent power in the western Mediterranean. On the morning after Cannae, the only Roman forces in the peninsula were the scattered remnants being collected by Varro, two legions of recruits at Rome, and another at Rome's coastal port, Ostia. Other legions were in north Italy (then the province of Cisalpine Gaul), Sicily and Sardinia – with the Cisalpine legions soon to be wiped out, too, in a Gallic ambush. We need not doubt that some of Hannibal's officers again urged him to march on Rome. As the senator and historian Cato, a young man in 216, was to tell it, Maharbal said: 'Send the cavalry with me: five days, and dinner will be cooked for you on the Capitol.' When Hannibal refused to be rushed, Maharbal famously replied – in Livy's version: 'True it is, the gods have not granted everything to the same man. You know how to win, Hannibal; you don't know how to exploit winning.'[15]

As mentioned above, Rome could not be reached from Cannae in five days and the story probably originated at Trasimene, only to become associated later with the greater victory. Maharbal, though, may well have proposed the same move now. Hannibal's refusal is generally considered sensible. His army was weary if not worn out, Rome lay 300 miles – fifteen to twenty days' march – across the hills and mountains, Saguntum had shown that he was not skilled at sieges, and the city still had defenders and functioning authorities. As effective master of south Italy, he soon began to attract defections, Capua among the first. Some months later he also won the Macedonian king, Philip V, as an ally and began to prise Syracuse from its friendship with Rome.

Maharbal's advice is not so easily discounted, all the same. The idea of immediately moving on Rome was valid, though this time he may not have asked to be sent ahead with the cavalry – that would have been worthwhile only from Trasimene. The fresh recruits at Rome would be bottled up inside the walls (if they emerged, their fate could be predicted); more important, so would the remaining Roman authorities, including what was left of the senate. Cut off from the rest of Italy, interdicted from supplies by land and water (for Hannibal could have blocked the Tiber), with their other troops too occupied or too shattered to bring rescue, their plight would have worsened fast. In other words, there was no need to try to storm one of the the world's largest and best fortified cities: it could have been blockaded, while the world, and Rome's wavering Italian allies, watched it starve.

Instead, as after Trasimene fourteen months earlier, Hannibal gave the Romans time and space to rebound. By spring 215, new levies rebuilt the legions to fourteen, 8 of them in the field in Italy (the same number as at Cannae) and all with matching allied contingents. Consuls and other magistrates were elected for 215, many of them former office-holders: one consul was Fabius. Another military commander was the formidable Marcus Claudius Marcellus, an ex-consul who would hold further consulships in years to come. From now on, the essentials of Fabius' strategy – avoiding battle but inflicting harassment – became the norm for all Roman commanders, and his once-disdainful nickname 'Delayer' became one of admiration. In the short run, as one city after another in southern Italy went over to the Carthaginians, this strategy had only an irritant impact. In the longer term, it proved the essential basis for Hannibal's defeat.

CHAPTER 5

HANNIBAL, CARTHAGE AND THE MEDITERRANEAN (216–209)

Hannibal in Campania and the South

Cannae was a revelation that seemed to announce a revolution. Not since Alexander the Great's time had an army in pitched battle so completely shattered another almost twice its size. Since Hannibal's arrival in Italy, over 85,000 Romans and their allies had perished – eleven per cent of all available manpower, according to the Romans' own figures. Few, if any, other generals could hope to match him in the field, and none could master him.

Hannibal expected the Romans to ask for negotiations. It was the obvious thing to do; if they fought on, he would defeat them again, and meanwhile more and more of their allies would be deserting them. Much of Italy, and some leaders outside, judged him both invincible and now worth backing. He himself wanted to make it clear that he had no wish to exterminate the enemy. He found and honourably buried the body of the fallen consul Aemilius Paullus; moreover, shortly after the battle,

he did something he had never done before: he summoned the

[captured] Romans and addressed them in gentle terms. His war with the Romans was not a fight to the death but a struggle for honour and power, he told them.[16]

He facilitated efforts for these prisoners to arrange for ransom, and with their emissaries to Rome he despatched one of his senior officers, Carthalo the cavalry general, to receive the overtures for peace.

Instead Carthalo was ordered out of Roman territory and, for the first time, all ransoming was refused. The Romans' implacability paradoxically went so far as to punish the survivors of Cannae. Reformed into two legions, they were sent to Sicily to serve until the war should end. In an earlier day, the Roman senate had resolved not to negotiate with Pyrrhus while he stood on Italian soil; during their earlier war with Carthage, even a series of naval disasters had not pushed them to offer talks; now they faced Hannibal with the same attitude. He must have been disappointed, but may not have been totally surprised – he knew recent history as well as anyone. What was necessary now, he evidently calculated, was to ratchet up the pressure, politically and militarily.

The first defectors were the Campanians of Capua, and some satellite towns of theirs. Wealthy, related to the Samnites of the highlands to their east, and resentful of a century's subordination to the Romans, the Capuan aristocracy struck an alliance with the victor and welcomed him into the city. His treaty with them set the standard for others in Italy and beyond: basically it stipulated that the Capuans were to be independent allies, and left open the issue of how extensively and in what ways they would participate in the war. According to Livy, Hannibal promptly abused the terms by ordering Capua's leading pro-Roman figure, Magius, to be arrested and put in chains aboard a ship for Carthage. Even if in reality he took care to work through the Capuan authorities, the story looks true in essentials: for stormy weather landed Magius at Cyrene instead, and he settled there under the protection of the king of Egypt – an unlikely coda for an anti-Hannibalic fiction. Still, Hannibal never repeated such a peremptory action.

Over the next several months, most of the Samnites, Lucanians and Bruttians also became allies; likewise important cities in Apulia such as Arpi, Herdonea and Salapia; and, among the southern Greek coastal cities, Locri and Croton. In practice, these alliances brought strains and problems as well as advantages. All of these states had been accustomed to supply regular contingents to the Romans' armies or fleets. Yet Hannibal seems to have made few if any similar arrangements; at least they are not stated in any of his reported treaties. Italians did join his forces: Bruttian troops are often mentioned, while his Samnite allies were soon complaining of being harassed by the Romans – 'you are not protecting us, and our own young men, who would be defending us if they were at home, are all serving in your forces.'[17] It looks as though Hannibal recruited Italians individually or by units into his own army on his own terms, like his Gauls, Spaniards and Numidians.

He could not afford to impose regular conscription, because unwilling recruits – and their home communities – could opt to defect back to the Romans. Capuan units did not figure at all in his field army, nor did soldiers of the Apulian towns or, later on, those of Greek allies such as Tarentum (Taranto) and Metapontum (Metaponto). These stayed home to protect their cities against the constant menace of Roman attacks. Yet local forces were often not strong enough to achieve this, especially with many men preferring to march with the Carthaginians. Threatened allies, like the unhappy Samnites, expected their powerful military patron to help. As time went by and the Romans learned the art of baffling him, such demands could conflict with Hannibal's own priorities.

Policies and priorities after Cannae

In spite of a few modern claims, his priorities did not include promoting democracy in Italy. We saw earlier how inaccurate it is to view him and his family as promoting democratic and anti-oligarchic government at home. Seeing Hannibal as democracy's champion in Italy rests on a disapproving remark of Livy's:

> it was as if a single disease had infected all the city-states of Italy: the commons were always in disagreement with the aristocrats, the senate favouring the Romans and the commons advocating a pro-Carthaginian policy.[18]

Livy repeatedly disproves his own claim – showing, for example, how at Capua, Locri, Arpi and Tarentum it was not the commons but their social superiors who took their cities into Hannibal's camp. Hannibal's many attractive qualities did not extend to egalitarianism. Nor did he give allies a voice in running the war: there was no general congress or conference, like the one Hasdrubal the elder had convened in Spain a decade earlier to be acclaimed supreme general. After all (as Hannibal might well point out) there was a war on, and it needed one unquestioned director. But, as we shall see, there were still other reasons for avoiding too much allied consultation.

After Cannae, the immediate priority was to win firm control of all Campania and to seize a port. Both proved impossible. South of his new ally, two other small towns, Nuceria and Acerrae, were sacked, but it took months to starve out the small town of Casilinum, guarding a major crossing over the Volturnus a few miles north-west of Capua. Marcellus drove back every assault on the stronghold of Nola, only 16 miles south-east of Capua across the plain. Attempts on Naples, Cumae nearby and later, during 214, Puteoli (Pozzuoli) were equally unsuccessful – and in that year Fabius recovered Casilinum.

These disappointments were not due to lack of troops. Certainly the original expeditionary personnel had shrunk, even if the heaviest losses had fallen on his Gallic soldiers who, on cold-blooded reckoning, were the most expendable; but Italian recruits were available in some numbers, as noted above. Indeed, Hannibal was soon strong enough to detach a force, first under his brother Mago and afterwards under their nephew Hanno, to win over most of the Samnites, and then the Bruttians and others in the south. Hanno, like the other senior officers in the army of invasion, was energetic and skilful (though he too was reduced to starving out, not storming, the stubborn little town of Petelia near Croton). He made his detached army into a significant force. Not only did he prompt much of the south to join the movement against Rome, but he was able in 215 to shepherd a welcome body of reinforcements north to Hannibal: 4,000 Numidian cavalry, forty elephants and a very large quantity of money. A year later Hanno was commanding a respectable army of 17,000 foot, chiefly Bruttians and Lucanians, together with 1,200 Numidian horse. Hannibal, operating in the main theatre, certainly had greater numbers. It is hard to see his own strength as under 50,000 infantry and cavalry – that is, the Cannae losses being at least replaced by Italian recruits – and quite possibly it was larger.

Nor was he out of touch with home. Besides the ship that sought to take Magius there, another ferried Mago over to report on Cannae to The Mighty Ones – famously pouring out a heap of gold rings at the senate's doorway, the spoil of thousands of dead Roman cavalrymen. The defection of ports on Italy's south coast made contact still easier: the reinforcements in 215 landed at Locri. It is surprising, then, that these reinforcements were so small – especially because, at the very same time, fresh armaments were sent from Carthage to Spain (where Hasdrubal suffered a defeat in 215 still worse than in 217) and Sardinia (where the

Carthaginians had incited a revolt against Roman rule): some 26,000 troops in all.

This disproportion between troop allocations is sometimes treated as more evidence for the home authorities being hostile to the Barcids. Yet the troops for Hasdrubal in Spain were under Mago's command and, in the forces for Sardinia, one of the officers was the brothers' close relative earlier mentioned, another Mago. Hannibal's brother, moreover, was originally commissioned at Carthage to take his forces to Italy; only the bad news from Spain prompted their diversion. Meanwhile Hannibal was sent plenty of money, possibly 1,000 talents, along with the Numidians and elephants. It is much likelier that all these troop movements were ordered by him, supervising the conduct of the war across Italy, Africa, Spain and the islands between, and more firmly than ever in control of overall affairs, thanks to Cannae.

The problems of partial success

Hannibal's later frustrations in Italy had other causes. As was becoming clear to everyone, he and his army were not good at capturing towns – least of all ones that mattered. This can only have improved the confidence of the communities that stayed loyal to the Romans: most notably the thirty Latin colonies. Many of these lay in the south, such as Beneventum, Luceria, Venusia and Brundisium, breaking up the continuity of territories allied with him. Meanwhile, the Romans' refusal either to negotiate or to accept another pitched battle threatened to consign him militarily to limbo. Another problem was that no other Carthaginian came even close to matching his generalship. Even Hanno proved all too easy for the enemy to beat, as they did in 214 by the river Calor near Beneventum, where all but a few thousand of his army were lost. The Romans had no first-class general either, but some commanders were more competent than most of his lieutenants. Tiberius Gracchus, for instance, defeated Hanno at the Calor, while Marcellus held his own against Hannibal himself, and soon to make an impact would be Quintus Fulvius Flaccus.

This drawback was equally serious outside Italy. In Spain Hannibal's brother Hasdrubal was an able administrator and popular commander, but suffered one blow after another at the hands of the Scipio brothers. The temporary best he could manage, after his defeat in 215, was to fend off further Roman progress southwards. Before long, the Barcids' political ally Hasdrubal son of Gisco would make an appearance, but he was little better at winning battles. At sea, as the navy built up, its most vigorous admiral was Bomilcar (the Barcids' brother-in-law?), but he too put up a sorry showing against enemy fleets. Nor did the war years bring any major new talent to the fore. Hannibal remained all that Carthage had. At Rome the situation would prove the opposite: one of the survivors of Cannae was the young officer Publius Cornelius Scipio, son of the general in Spain.

Directly after Cannae, none of these problems made themselves obvious. The defections of the Capuans and other Italian states not only deprived the enemy of military manpower – the consul Varro reckoned the Campanians' manpower alone at 34,000 – but formed the alliance system which Hannibal and Carthage needed for permanent hegemony in Italy. It was vital not simply to force the Romans to terms, but to create a situation which would lastingly favour Carthage. The more bonds Hannibal could form with ex-Roman allies, the weaker and more hemmed-in Rome would be after the war, and the stronger Punic dominance would be. Waiting for the enemy to seek terms, and simultaneously gathering Italian states into alliance, were thus two sides to the same coin.

Yet this goal implied another potential problem for Hannibal. The Capuans almost certainly expected to replace Rome as the dominant

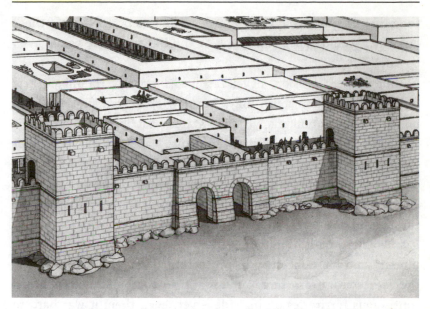

An artist's reconstruction of the sea-wall of Carthage. Carthage was
renowned for her powerful fortifications. Reproduced from M.H. Fantar,
Carthage: la Cité punique (Paris and Tunis, 1995), by kind permission of
CNRS Éditions, Paris.

Italian power. There was no place in such a scenario for Carthaginian
hegemony. Of course, what the Capuans thought right and proper
for themselves was not likely to persuade Samnites, Bruttians and
Italian Greeks; these would scarcely revolt from Roman dominance
in order to pass under Capua's. But Punic hegemony was not
something for Hannibal to proclaim – especially as it could not
last without a permanent Punic military presence. If he simply cut
back the Roman state – for instance, to its size a century and a half
before – and then withdrew, as the Capuans (and probably others)
expected him to do, Italy would swiftly fall back into its age-old
pattern of endlessly warring states. Eventually one of them – maybe
even Rome again – would come to dominate the rest; or Macedon,

the other neighbouring great power, would step in. None of these outcomes would benefit Carthage or the Barcids; none would even be safe.

Thus a latent tension, never resolved, underlay Hannibal's new order in central and south Italy. The new order had another, more immediate limitation: many Italian states' stubborn loyalty to their old leader. No Latin colony budged; Nola, Naples and several other Campanian cities stood firm; so too, in Samnium, the big canton of the Pentri; among the Greek cities, Tarentum, Metapontum and Thurii for some years after 216, and Cumae, Naples and Rhegium throughout the war. Hannibal's new alliance system remained in patches like a quilt, reinforcing the individual states' sense of self-interest and his difficulties in protecting them. Only after 212 in the deep south, from Tarentum around to Locri, did he have broad continuous territories on his side – yet, even then, it was hard to prevent Roman forces moving where they wished, unless he himself marched against them.

The treaty with Macedon

Distracting the Romans with worries outside Italy was, therefore, another goal. Philip V of Macedon was easily enticed, for he had interests in Illyria's coastlands where the Romans exercised a fairly light hegemony. Hannibal made contact with him, and Polybius quotes the Greek text of the sworn treaty of 215 which sealed their alliance (it fell into the Romans' hands). Hannibal very possibly drafted it himself, for some of its phrases are echoed in much older Phoenician and Hittite pacts. At all events, this is the nearest we come to Hannibal in his own voice.

On his side, the oath is sworn not only by Hannibal himself but by 'Mago [the Samnite?], Myrcan, Barmocar [both unknown; either officers of his or envoys from Carthage], such members of the

Carthaginian senate as were present, and all Carthaginians serving in his army'; on the other side, by Philip's chief envoy Xenophanes. The text then names or describes all the gods and goddesses invoked as witnesses (including 'all the gods of those on campaign'), and applies its provisos to all the cities and peoples allied to either side – among them 'the people of Utica' and 'all cities and tribes in Italy, Gaul, and Liguria' on current or future terms of 'friendship and alliance' with Carthage. The two sides swear to 'support and protect' each other, and have the same enemies 'excepting those kings, cities, and ports with which we have sworn agreements and friendships'. Then come more specific clauses:

> You shall be friends to us in the war in which we now are engaged against the Romans, till such time as the gods give us and you the victory: and you shall assist us in all ways that be needful, and in whatsoever way we may mutually determine.
>
> And when the gods have given you and us victory in our war with the Romans and their allies, if the Romans decide to negotiate friendship, these terms shall include the same friendship with you, made on these conditions: the Romans not to be allowed in any way to make war on you; not to have control of Corcyra, Apollonia, Epidamnus, Pharos, Dimale, Parthini, nor Atintania; to restore to Demetrius of Pharos all those of his friends now in the dominion of Rome [Demetrius, an Illyrian opponent of Rome's, had fled to Philip for protection]. If the Romans ever make war on you or on us we will aid each other in such war, according to the need of either.

They also promise the same mutual aid in any future war against other states, 'always excepting kings, cities, and tribes with whom we have sworn agreements and friendships'.[19]

What is striking, apart from the fact that the only territorial adjustments mentioned concern places of interest to Philip, is

how Hannibal and the Carthaginians take it for granted that a
Roman state will still exist after the war – in fact will still have the
capacity to wage future wars, even against Macedon or Carthage.
The treaty thus implicitly forecasts ongoing tension between victors
and defeated. It was an inevitable forecast if Hannibal planned to
maintain a Punic hegemony in Italy, without reducing the Roman
state to a nonentity. At the same time, paradoxically, he may well
have seen this as a desirable outcome – for a shrunken yet still
vigorous, and potentially combative, Rome would further justify a
continuing Carthaginian presence in Italy.

It is not likely that this implicit forecast was mere disinformation
to divert Philip from suspecting that Hannibal really planned the
total subjugation of Italy. Both leaders knew well enough that no
implied assurance about Rome continuing to exist would count if
a genuine prospect arose of destroying her completely. In other
words, adding such a clause in hopes of deluding the other signatory
would have been pointless. Instead, Philip's willingness to make the
treaty suggests that, like Hannibal, he expected the most realistic
outcome of the war to be a comprehensive Roman defeat, but not
the annihilation of Rome. From his point of view, he now had a
unique opportunity for acquiring control of the Adriatic coasts
and islands, assured of the cordial support of the new hegemon of
Italy.

Philip V was surely astute enough to realise that replacing Roman
hegemony with Carthage's was no guarantee of endless peaceful
coexistence. The great war in the west was watched with fascination,
and some concern, by the states of the east: for it was obvious
that whoever won would dominate the western Mediterranean
– and would turn eastwards sooner or later. At a peace conference
in Greece in 217, one delegate warned his perpetually bickering
countrymen to pay attention to this: 'for if once you allow the
clouds now gathering in the west to settle upon Greece, I fear

exceedingly that the power of making peace or war, and in a word all these games which we are now playing against each other, will be completely knocked out of the hands of us all.'[20] In 215 the coming victor, it seemed clear, would be Carthage under Hannibal. Had this come true, then the interventions in Greece that the Romans were to initiate after the Second Punic War might well have occurred under Hannibal's leadership, and the resulting Roman hegemony over the east would have been Carthaginian and Barcid.

Hannibal at the zenith

Sicily, too, offered prospects for widening the war to the enemy's disadvantage. The independent kingdom of Syracuse was a loyal Roman ally so long as its aged ruler Hiero lived, but hostile feeling ran through much of the population and even through the royal family. When Hiero's grandson Hieronymus succeeded to the throne in 215, this feeling began to emerge, as the boy king's dominant councillors thought it an ideal moment to reclaim Syracuse's old supremacy in the island. To do so meant allying with Carthage: contact was duly made with Hannibal. He sent over another Hannibal, probably his friend 'the Gladiator', as his agent and with him two brothers, Hippocrates and Epicydes, of part-Syracusan and part-Carthaginian parentage. A fateful alliance between Syracuse and Carthage was struck. The two brothers turned out to be more than ordinarily adroit activists in the upheavals that followed, when Hieronymus' capriciousness, and Syracusan aristocrats' conflicting ambitions, caused his assassination in 214 in favour of a republic with pro-Roman as well as pro-Carthaginian factions. The Roman commanders in Sicily, Marcellus and Appius Claudius, naturally backed the pro-Roman group, but Hippocrates and Epicydes overcame all setbacks to become elected Syracusan generals and uphold the new alliance.

Hannibal had further geopolitical concerns. As noted earlier, he had to attend to the needs of Punic Spain, where his brother Hasdrubal and his colleagues were hard pressed by the Scipio brothers. Sardinia, roused to revolt by a Carthaginian agent, was also sent help, though unsuccessfully. North Africa itself suffered intermittent damage and terror from Roman raiding fleets. The needs of the war required a sizeable increase in the Punic navy, from the 87 warships ready for action in 218 to the 130 reported in Sicilian waters six years later. Hannibal, no seaman himself, almost certainly entrusted the details of this expansion to the Barcid home authorities.

For the same reasons too, the artificial ports in the southern sector of Carthage may have been constructed in these years – the outer merchant port, and the inner port for a 200-ship navy. Not only did the navy grow but there is no sign, either, of Carthage's maritime trade being severely curtailed during most of the war. Presumably her trade with Roman-controlled Italy was lost, though even this cannot be certain. Still, her closer ties with southern Italy after 216 may well have boosted that rich region's trade with North Africa. Shipping, in turn, needed protection from Roman coastal raids: that could explain the merchant port being included. By contrast, if the two havens had been built earlier, between the first and second wars with Rome, the meagreness of the navy in 218 is impossible to explain. The real problem is that nearly all the datable archaeological remains are from the 150s, but it may be that the ports were totally overhauled then for the benefit of Carthage's flourishing maritime commerce.

In 215 and 214 Hannibal's and Carthage's star was at its zenith. Much of southern Italy was in their camp, and likewise Macedon and Syracuse. Gallic north Italy was a pro-Punic bastion. Hasdrubal in Spain, despite defeats, brought the Scipio brothers to a stalemate that lasted nearly three years. The military initiative was principally

Barcid coin of Hannibal's time, New Carthage *c.* 221–209 BC. A very fine silver dishekel (coin holed above). *Obverse*: male head with wreath to right (Melqart?), club behind. *Reverse*: elephant walking to right. Photograph provided by courtesy of Noble Numismatics Ltd., Sydney, from the collection of Dr Stephen Mulligan.

in Carthaginian hands, with the Romans forced into mainly defensive reactions: for instance to Hannibal's attacks on pro-Roman places in Campania, to Hanno's activities in south Italy, and to Carthaginian intervention in Sardinia and Sicily. The Carthaginians were putting as great an effort into the war as their enemies, with Hannibal's two armies in Italy, his garrisons in key allied Italian cities, his brother Hasdrubal's forces in Spain, the expeditionary armament to Sardinia, and the troops protecting Carthage and Punic Africa. Altogether these land forces must have totalled at least 150,000, the navy another 30,000 and rising. The Romans had about the same numbers under arms across all fronts.

By 214 Hannibal had achieved most of what he had planned in 218. After Cannae, final victory and lasting supremacy seemed within Carthage's grasp. The Romans and their remaining allies were boxed in geographically by Carthaginian forces or allies. The wealth of Spain and Punic Africa paid for the war without, it seems, as yet putting heavy burdens on the state. The republic, which in past centuries' wars had found it hard to cope with the Sicilian Greeks alone, was the greatest power in the western Mediterranean and the potential equal of those east of the Adriatic. This was largely Hannibal's doing, backed by his energetic family and political allies, and by his devoted armies.

Operational lifestyles

Hannibal's lifestyle in Italy, and that of his hard-working soldiers, followed a regular rhythm: vigorous campaigning in central and southern Italy between about March and November, then a winter recess. Major battles, epic sieges and bold strategic thrusts did occur but were few, though dangers and action aplenty remained. Pro-Carthaginian Italy was nowhere more than 250 miles wide, and nearly all the Italian warfare after Cannae was concentrated there, in the arc from Capua to Bruttium. The winter recess, even in southern Italy, was practically essential: armies were more or less permanently in being but were especially difficult to provision between November and March. After wintering in 216 at Capua (with dire impact, in legend anyway, on the army's appetite for war) Hannibal and his men spent most ensuing winters in Apulia or nearby: at Arpi in 215, in 214 at Salapia, down in the heel of Italy the following winter, and from then on mostly in Lucania or Bruttium.

Unlike Alexander the Great, Hannibal was noted for neither drinking-carousals nor high living – nor for tyrannical excesses like the burning of a Persepolis or the murder of an old friend at dinner. The generalised portrayals of him in Livy and others would suit his life in Italy as suitably as Spain:

He could be physically exhausted or mentally cowed by no hardship [Livy writes]. He had the ability to withstand heat and cold alike; his eating and drinking depended on the requirements of nature, not pleasure. His times for being awake and asleep were not determined by day or night. To sleep was given only the time he had left from discharging his duties, and it was not brought on by a soft bed or silence – many often observed him lying on the ground, amidst the sentry-posts and pickets, wrapped in a soldier's cloak. His dress was no better than that of his comrades, but his weapons and horses marked him out.

In Dio's epigram, 'hardship made him rugged, and on loss of sleep he grew strong.' Perhaps he did relax somewhat during a quiet winter; a couple of writers mention that, during the winter of 211–210 at Salapia, he had a well-publicised affair with a mistress, presumably a local lady. It would hardly be surprising for an active man in his thirties, far from home and family.[21]

He did commit acts of harshness, but some of those reported look like enemy inventions – such as the notorious bridge of corpses he supposedly used to march over a river, or the Campanian guide in 216 crucified for misunderstanding his Punic pronunciation of a town he wanted to reach. After a prominent man of Arpi, Dasius, defected in 213, Hannibal (according to Livy) punished his wife and children by burning them alive – a unique act of transferred savagery, or another Roman atrocity story? Other acts which do look genuine he no doubt justified as military necessities. On the march down the Adriatic coast after Trasimene, every able-bodied male the army found was killed as being a Roman enemy; and in his move on Tarentum in 212, his Numidian scouts were ordered to kill any peasants they met, to prevent word of his approach. Sacking captured towns was normal in a war, as was selling prisoners into slavery, and Hannibal certainly did both. All the same, we must sprinkle a pinch of salt over Appian's claim – often described, inaccurately, as Hannibal's boast – that over fifteen years in Italy he destroyed 400 cities and slew 300,000 people.[22]

Hannibal took good care of his troops. Our sources emphasise their devotion, though they are too sweeping in insisting that he never suffered a desertion (several are reported, and by 211 there were over a thousand Numidian cavalry turncoats quartered at Rome). The enthusiasm and loyalty of the great majority of his troops was the more striking because, as Polybius and others point out, under his standards he had men from all over the Mediterranean. In battles, his losses were nearly always much less than the enemy's; in commissariat, we hear only occasionally of hardship – notably over winter 217–216 and, much later, in the bad harvest year of 205. But the ordinary attrition of war took its toll on his original Spanish, African and Gallic units: as already mentioned, we read more and more of Italian contingents in his forces. Bruttians were particularly notable.

How he organised supplies and, just as crucially, funds for his armies can only be surmised, but it is clear that his troops seldom had grounds for complaint. The reputation for greed that Polybius mentions (and Livy is keen to stress) may, at least in part, be due to his concern always to have money to pay them; he could remember how the 'Truceless War' of his father's time had stemmed from the grievances of unpaid men. Funds were sent to him from Carthage in 215, perhaps too on other, unmentioned occasions (they needed less shipping than troop reinforcements). But the bulk of his finances in Italy must have come from local sources: erratically, from looting and the sale of prisoners (sources whose yield would lessen over the years); more regularly through allies' contributions – if these did occur, without being noticed in our sources. That he suffered no mutinies, and no unusual level of desertions, even in the later and defensive years in Italy is another tribute to his powers of leadership.

The Romans fight back

Setbacks did occur, even early on. The expedition to Sardinia in 215 came to grief and his kinsman Mago was one of those captured. In the following year, an attempt by Hannibal to capture Tarentum was foiled, Fabius Maximus recaptured Casilinum near Capua, and Tiberius Gracchus defeated Hanno's southern army by the river Calor. There were disappointments overseas: Philip V's operations in Illyria were humiliatingly frustrated by Roman forces which, in a night attack on his sleeping camp, put him to flight in his underwear. More ominously Marcellus, Rome's most combative general, joined Appius Claudius in Sicily and began to win successes against the Syracusans. In North Africa itself, relations with the ambitious western Numidian king, Syphax, worsened until fighting broke out, for his ambition was to take over eastern Numidia – dispossessing its pro-Carthaginian (and Barcid-related) rulers – and the Romans were naturally glad to send him help. This was one distraction which Carthage was able to settle by 210, with Syphax pacified by Hasdrubal son of Gisco but the eastern king, old Gaia, still in place.

Resourceful as the Carthaginians were, their opponents matched them step for step. True to the spirit of Fabian tactics, they avoided battle with Hannibal himself and tackled his subordinates and allies (a tactic that Napoleon's enemies in turn were to apply in 1813). The result overall was an impasse in the war, though individual gains and losses occurred. Hannibal was undefeatable in the field and still capable of a brilliant coup such as the seizure of Tarentum in 212, but the offensive drive of the first three years inevitably slowed. In such theatres as Illyria, Sicily and then Spain, the Romans were soon on the offensive, and their opponents – Carthaginian or allied – found it hard to cope.

Strategically the war after 216 until about 211 was, in effect, an arms-length siege of Rome – the Carthaginians putting pressure at every available point in Italy and outside, the Romans counter-attacking in some areas and simply holding tight in others. Campania was the focus in 215 and 214. As mentioned above, Hannibal's attempts on Nola were repelled by the indefatigable Marcellus, Gracchus routed Hanno, and Fabius retook Casilinum. Then in 213 the Romans won back Arpi in Apulia; on the other hand Hanno and a newly recruited army made short work of an irregular force of enemy partisans in Bruttium.

Over in Sicily, Syracuse's brief dream of renewed empire vanished when Marcellus, with the survivors of Cannae as his army, mopped up the countryside and put the city itself under siege. Archimedes' defence-machines only postponed the inevitable. Yet another Punic army was sent over from Africa under a Himilco, one no less than 28,000 strong and with a dozen elephants, but Himilco made little impact and finally perished in an epidemic with most of his men. Late in 212, treachery opened Syracuse's gates to Marcellus. This knocked away one of the overseas levers which Hannibal had meant to use against the Romans, though it did not directly constrain his own efforts in Italy.

The march on Rome

Successes and frustrations also occurred in 212 in Italy. Hannibal's coup in taking Tarentum, the leading Greek city and port in the south-east, was limited by the Romans' continuing occupation of its citadel, which commanded the harbour. Still, after Tarentum he won other Greek cities down the coast – Metapontum, Heraclea and Thurii – which had till now stayed loyal to Rome. This left only Rhegium (Reggio) at the toe of the peninsula on the enemy's side.

On the other hand, this extension of Punic allied territory did not force the Romans back on the defensive. By this time they had no fewer than twenty-five legions in arms: ten of them along the fronts from Campania to Bruttium, another four in Etruria and north Italy, and the rest in Sicily, Spain, Sardinia and the Adriatic. In fact, about one adult man in four of the Roman and allied population was on military or naval service in 212. The new consuls, Fulvius Flaccus and Appius Claudius, took the fateful initiative to move on Capua, would-be capital of a liberated Italy. When Hanno marched up from the south, Fulvius stormed his camp near Beneventum and drove him back south. The Roman siege-lines around Capua were so strong that Hannibal himself found it impossible to break through, despite pleas and recriminations from the besieged. It was small consolation, instead, to destroy another irregular enemy force in Lucania over the mountains sixty miles away, or even to catch the Roman army in Apulia and wipe it out – 16,000 dead or captured – in a classic ambush near Herdonea (Ordona). For the Romans it was worth the two defeats, and worth even the death of Gracchus afterwards in a Lucanian skirmish, to remove Hannibal from the scene for the rest of the year while they tightened the siege further. His movements in 212, therefore, amounted to a serious miscalculation or, at least, a bad choice of priorities.

When he returned early in 211 to the heights above Capua, he found six legions investing the city and all prospect of forcing a relief gone. As with so many cities, so too with siegeworks: they were outside even his capabilities. The Romans kept within them and refused to come out. Polybius sums up the problem:

> I think the reason of the strategy adopted by the two sides respectively was that they both had seen that Hannibal's cavalry was the main cause of the Carthaginian victory and Roman defeat. ... For the Roman army did not venture to come out and give battle, from fear of the enemy's horse, but remained resolutely within their entrenchment; well knowing that the

cavalry, by which they had been worsted in the battles, could not hurt them there.[23]

This realisation had seriously bad implications for the Carthaginians. If the enemy were to adopt a similar method with other allied cities, it would require much time and cost but Hannibal's laboriously gained territorial base could be sequentially amputated, while he watched impotently from the sidelines.

It was five years since Cannae. No more defections were likely unless he could revitalise the war in the field – or inflict some other master-stroke on the enemy. It was now that he decided to execute his famous march on Rome.

The aim of this manoeuvre was to draw enough Roman forces away from Capua to make it impossible to continue the siege, and also, Polybius states, because 'he might, by the alarm which he would inspire in the inhabitants by his unexpected movement, perhaps do something worthwhile against the city itself.'[24] Better still, if the besiegers divided their forces, he could defeat each in turn. Thus occurred the advance against his enemies' capital which he should have carried out five or, indeed, six years before. The fear and even panic it aroused in the city were severe (a token of what would have happened in the still more desperate days after Trasimene or Cannae): yet the manoeuvre misfired completely.

The authorities in Rome kept their nerve. There were new levies in the city, and as many as 1,200 Numidian deserters willing to fight. According to Livy, Fulvius also led back a body of troops from Campania by forced marches. Hannibal plundered and laid waste the countryside round about, but could not compel a battle. Not because the Romans cowered behind their walls – they emerged and pitched camp little more than a mile from him. They did not offer battle, and he refused the risk of attacking their camp. Perhaps he feared that a sortie from the city could take him at a disadvantage.

Instead, laden with plunder, the Carthaginians moved off, at first under harassment from the enemy until Hannibal drove them off with a night attack. He then tried to salvage the operation by marching swiftly (though it must still have taken about three weeks) right down the peninsula in a thrust at Rhegium; but this failed too. Worst of all, the starving Capuans had no option left but to capitulate to their besiegers.

The tide begins to ebb

The fall of Capua and its satellite towns, which led to harsh punishments for rebel leaders and citizens, forced the Carthaginians back into southern Italy. Salapia, another Apulian stronghold, rejoined the Romans in 210. The Samnites were a lost cause: during 210 they wilted under more Roman assaults, and the following year those who remained in arms surrendered. The fall of Syracuse released Marcellus, the most aggressive general on the enemy's side, to hold a fourth consulship in 210, this time with south Italy as his theatre. This reinforced the reversal in momentum that had begun in 212 with the siege of Capua.

From now on, Hannibal, though often aggressive tactically, was strategically on the defensive. He was still agilely unpredictable: in 210, once more near Herdonea in Apulia, he surprised and shattered a Roman army in the classic way, holding the enemy infantry with his own while his cavalry galloped around to strike from the rear. Thousands of men, including their commander, were killed. Not long afterwards, he fought a day-long battle with Marcellus at Numistro in Lucania (Muro Lucano, north-west of Potenza), then broke away eastwards during the night. In essence, though, this was all done to hold on to the territories that he had won after Cannae. Watched constantly by two or more enemy armies spread out across the south, having to beat back Roman incursions or attacks on his allies, he was never again able to break out of that quarter of Italy to range freely and widely, as in the great days of Trasimene and Cannae. With Sicily lost by 210, and the momentum gone from Philip V's war across the Adriatic, his one remaining strategy for final victory was to hold on as strongly as possible in Italy until powerful reinforcements could arrive, this time from Spain.

The Romans' renewed combativeness from 212 on had extended to Spain, where after some years' inactivity the brothers Publius and Gnaeus Scipio launched a fresh offensive into the south. Obscure though the details are (Livy dates them wrongly to 214, no doubt like his sources, and has little clear idea of the places involved), the brothers made serious inroads into the far south, enough to allow them to winter at and near Castulo – the home town of Hannibal's wife – which must now have thought them the winning side. Then in 211 they over-confidently divided their forces for quicker progress. In fact they were faced not only by Hasdrubal, the middle Barcid, but by his brother Mago and Hasdrubal son of Gisco, a close political ally of the family though not (it seems) a kinsman. With them, as commander of their Numidian cavalry, they had Masinissa, son of old Gaia the eastern Numidian king. The Numidian prince to whom Hamilcar had once promised a daughter as wife may have been Masinissa's uncle and, if so, he too had links with the Barcid family. These leaders overcame first Publius' and then Gnaeus' widely separated forces, four weeks apart, killing both brothers and most of their men. It was the greatest Punic victory in the field since Cannae, and Punic Spain was saved.

Hannibal's grand strategy envisaged his brother Hasdrubal marching from Spain in his footsteps to Italy. With fresh Spanish and African troops and fresh Gallic auxiliaries arriving, this would revitalise the war. It would be the brothers' turn to lead a super-army against the Romans: one that could sweep aside or pulverise any opposition and at last fix a grip of iron around Rome.

No thought was ever given, it seems, to the alternative of reinforcing Hannibal by sea. This was strange, for not only had the Numidians and elephants in 215 arrived that way, thanks to Bomilcar the admiral, but until 210 Punic armies – cavalry and elephants included – regularly fared by ship to Sicily. Even afterwards the Punic navy continued to be active, though with little success: in 208 a fleet, eighty-three strong, confronted Roman raiders on the African coast (only to be defeated), while in 209 and again in 207 another fleet operated (futilely) in Greek waters. Later still, both the Roman invasion of Africa in 204, and Hannibal's own return with his troops in 203, were necessarily by water. The only explanation, but a not entirely satisfactory one, is that Hannibal would not risk reinforcements being caught and destroyed at sea. He saw a lesser risk in Hasdrubal marching from Spain to north Italy, and then down through the peninsula, to join him.

Supposedly, Hasdrubal had been ordered to march as long ago as 215 – but whatever the accuracy of that report, he certainly had the opportunity in 211 after annihilating the Scipios. All that stood between him and north Italy were the remnants of their forces, which he allowed to retreat to the dubious safety of north-eastern Spain. Then, perhaps because of wrangles between the two brothers and also with Hasdrubal son of Gisco, nobody did anything. Yet the destruction of the Scipios could have counter-balanced the fall of Capua if it had been fully exploited, and we can be sure it would have been if Hannibal had been there. The three generals' inactivity is both inexplicable and inexcusable. It illustrates, too, a decline in Hannibal's previously unquestioned grip on all Carthaginian affairs. He could not discipline even his two brothers' feuding – still less prod Hasdrubal into making the move to Italy in 211 or 210. This was not from lack of communi-cations with Spain, which could be maintained via Carthage, even if it took time. Rather, he could no longer impose his will on them at long range. They had won a great victory, he had lost Campania.

It is not the only item that points to a decline in his authority. When still another Punic army went from Africa to Sicily in 210, he seconded to it Mottones of Hippacra, one of his trusted cavalry officers. Mottones' dash and determination – and half-Libyan race – turned the Punic commander Himilco against him despite his credentials. Finally the exasperated Hippacritan defected to the Romans, who welcomed him with open arms (and made him a citizen). Again, the overall stalemate within Italy not only caused some of the new allies to give up, but encouraged even some significant desertions among Hannibal's own men. As mentioned earlier, in 211 there were reportedly as many as 1,200 renegade Numidian cavalrymen quartered in Rome. In Sicily, too, by 209 the Romans had a sizeable division of Numidian deserter cavalry and infantry in their forces. Yet cavalry – Numidian cavalry especially – was the arm he could least afford to lose. Most of his Numidians remained fiercely loyal, as, for instance, the 500 garrisoning Salapia who nearly all fought to the death when the townsfolk let the Romans in; but others had clearly grown disenchanted with the long war and with their leader.

Hannibal versus Marcellus

The war situation, by 210, stood at a dangerous equilibrium. Hannibal could hold his own in Italy, but without a major victory his position could not last indefinitely. In Spain, Hasdrubal and his colleagues did not follow up their great victory. Meanwhile Roman raids resumed against North Africa's coasts, a new commander was appointed to Spain – the 25-year-old Publius Scipio, son and nephew of the lately slain generals – and Marcellus in south Italy adopted a pugnacious yet calculated method for confronting Hannibal himself.

Previous Roman generals, as we have seen, had avoided him and attacked his allies and subordinates. Marcellus, confident in the stamina and experience of his long-serving legions, was prepared to hazard battle. The result was indecisive clashes at Numistro in 210 and Canusium (Canosa) in 209, in each of which he seems to have fared worse than Hannibal, yet remained in possession of the field while it was Hannibal who retired. After Numistro, indeed, Marcellus pursued him closely, harassing his columns and provoking costly skirmishes. Hannibal could replace his losses with more Italian levies, but such campaigns of attrition were bound to wear down his prestige, resources and authority even further.

Marcellus' methods were a good deal more sophisticated than the unsubtle confrontations that had led to Trebia, Trasimene and Cannae, and a good deal more venturesome – though much riskier – than those of Fabius and other commanders between 215 and 211. There was still another drawback for Hannibal: while he scrapped unproductively with Marcellus, other Roman forces in south Italy could act. In 209 Fabius Maximus (consul for the fifth time) ordered a thrust from Rhegium on Caulonia in Bruttium. When Hannibal broke away from Marcellus in Apulia to save Caulonia, Fabius executed a feat entirely Hannibalic in style by capturing Tarentum through internal treachery. Hannibal is supposed to have commented sourly, 'The Romans have their Hannibal, too; we have lost Tarentum the same way we took it', and to have been depressed enough to tell his closest friends that there was no prospect now of mastering Italy.[25] All this was rather too generous to Fabius, whose only coup of the kind it was, but it acknowledged a deeper truth. In adapting Fabius' original methods of delay, harassment and distraction, Roman commanders as a group were matching Hannibal's own mastery of strategy and tactics. Hannibal soon rebounded from his gloom, but for any remaining hope of victory it was now imperative that Hasdrubal should march from Spain.

CHAPTER 6

DECLINE AND DEFEAT (209–202)

Failures and successes in 209–208

The year 209 was the turning point in the Second Punic War. Not only did the Romans retake Tarentum and force most of the Samnites to capitulate, but the new commander in Spain – young Publius Scipio – confounded the Carthaginians by leading his forces from north-eastern Spain to capture New Carthage itself. This extraordinary coup took advantage of the continuing dissensions between all three Punic generals in Spain, Hannibal's two brothers and Hasdrubal son of Gisco, and their shared contempt for the remnant of Roman troops around Tarraco. They had located their troops in widely separated regions, none near New Carthage (Mago, for example, was wintering by the Atlantic), and had left barely 1,000 regular troops in the capital of Punic Spain. A day after his arrival there, Scipio stormed the city and completely changed the prospects of the war.

Scipio was a phenomenon new to the conflict: a Roman leader in Hannibal's own class. This was not yet obvious, but his coup at New Carthage was a portent that Hannibal could not fail to recognise. Not only was it a major prize, not only did it put the Carthaginians in Spain totally on the defensive: it implied something much worse.

If the Romans could keep Hannibal in Italy, slowly losing ground to the Marcellan version of Fabian strategy while they operated aggressively outside, then Africa and Carthage were in mortal danger, and Hannibal would be powerless to save them. To turn the war around, he had to have the new forces from Spain.

The advent of Scipio made this still harder to achieve. Hasdrubal had not marched in 215 nor in 211. He now had to defend the Punic – and Barcid – province of Spain with minimal assistance from his brother Mago and the son of Gisco. Why all three were so mutually uncooperative, in the face of the menace from Scipio, is hard to understand, especially as they had done the opposite with total success against his father and uncle in 211. Two could have kept him in play while the third made for Italy undisturbed. Instead, Hasdubal was left on his own, to fight Scipio first and then try to leave for Italy. He did in fact do both, though the battle of Baecula (near Bailén) in the south in 208 was a heavy defeat that cost men and time. Scipio let him go, for there were still his colleagues to deal with. Just as relevant, Scipio could read Italian geography perfectly well.

Hasdrubal, popular and a good planner, reorganised and re-expanded his army, crossed the Pyrenees late in 208 – and then passed the winter in southern Gaul. This was yet another curious decision, for in south Italy that year Hannibal won his last notable successes. His Numidians ambushed both consuls, Marcellus and Crispinus, when they incautiously rode out with only a small escort to reconnoitre ground. Marcellus was killed, Crispinus so badly wounded that he died later in the year. As Livy caustically remarks:

> [Marcellus] had blindly thrown himself, his colleague and, one might almost say, the entire republic into a reckless situation, and that was not in keeping with his age – he was then more

than sixty – or the caution one would have expected from a veteran commander.

Hannibal admired Marcellus: according to Plutarch, he said that he respected Fabius as a teacher but Marcellus as an opponent. He gave the dead consul honourable burial, just as he had Paullus after Cannae and Gracchus in 210; in one account, preserved by Plutarch again, he cremated the body and sent the ashes to Marcellus' son.[26]

At the same time, he followed up the coup by making an attempt to recapture Salapia. This failed due to Crispinus' precautions, so he promptly struck south to rescue Locri, garrisoned by his friend Mago the Samnite, from a Roman attack led by Cincius Alimentus, the future historian who later became his prisoner. His skill and dash were still very evident. Moreover some aristocratic circles in Etruria were restive under Roman hegemony, and Roman forces in the north were limited. Had Hasdrubal arrived in Italy during 208, amid the dismay and temporary disarray of the enemy, he would have made more of an impact on events than he was to do in 207, when they had regrouped. As it was, the new invasion was so widely signalled ahead that they had time to reinforce the northern front with a consul's army, and take steps to contain Hannibal in the south.

Hannibal's lethal ambush may also have won him a lesser success at the cost of a bigger, for Marcellus and Crispinus had been looking for a pitched battle. There is no certainty that he would have beaten them, but he would surely have had a good chance, whereas the dying Crispinus took steps to prevent any further clashes. Nevertheless, the momentous year 207 put that missed chance in the shade. It featured a disturbing litany of miscalculations and hesitations – many of them by Hannibal himself – and ended in his brother's destruction.

Hasdrubal invades Italy

Hasdrubal, without losing a man, reached north Italy over the Alps in spring. Once Gallic recruits joined him, he had some 30,000 men. Yet he was 450 miles from Lucania and Bruttium. Fifteen Roman legions stood between him and Hannibal. The obvious goal was for the two to unite their armies, so Hasdrubal sent off horsemen with a despatch to his brother proposing a junction in Umbria, the region about 100 miles north of Rome.

In the same spring, Hannibal was performing a series of manoeuvres in the south which are difficult to make sense of from Livy's account (our one source). We should expect him to be seeking to break away from the forces shadowing him, so as to march north. But, as Livy tells it, he first moved into the heel of Italy, then shifted over to Bruttium, next swung north-eastwards through Lucania into Apulia; after that, south again to Metapontum, and finally northwards to Canusium where he stopped, still hundreds of miles from Hasdrubal. These manoeuvres were frustratingly zigzag and truncated if his goal was central or northern Italy.

One reason must be that at every stage he was followed by the enemy. The southern command was under the new consul Gaius Claudius Nero, who twice engaged him: once in Lucania at Grumentum (Grumento Nova, south of Potenza) and then at Venusia (Venosa) in Apulia. Both battles were indecisive, but they slowed the Carthaginian army and cost it casualties: attrition-style warfare again. Tellingly, Hannibal's detour to Metapontum after the second battle was to pick up fresh troops recruited by his nephew Hanno. The Romans' persistence seems to have drained him of further initiative beyond Canusium. The days of swift and unexpected moves to elude a baffled enemy were gone; perhaps too many of his current troops were inexperienced levies. Perhaps, also, some of his Bruttians and Lucanians were restive at any prospect of leaving their own region behind to the unhindered attention of the Romans, and he could no longer afford to compel them.

He did not receive Hasdrubal's despatch, because the bearers – after getting as far as Metapontum and finding him gone – were captured by the enemy. Yet he himself made no effort to try contacting his brother. If everything hinged on a single letter being delivered, after a 400-mile journey through Italy by six foreign riders (Hasdrubal presumably distrusted Italian deserters as messengers), this was a disastrous mistake. Plainly nothing had been arranged earlier between the brothers, for instance during the previous year, and now each had to act by intuition. Hasdrubal was left with the task of marching to Hannibal down the geographic length of Italy through unfamiliar hills, valleys and mountains, confronted by Roman forces all the way and at risk of finding himself surrounded, while his brother and superior commander stayed encamped in Apulia. Hannibal was probably awaiting word from Hasdrubal or other sources (deserters, for instance) that would clarify matters before he made his next move: a safe enough plan, once upon a time. This time he was outmanoeuvred by the Romans.

The consul Nero's performance so far in the war had been unspectacular. His most notable service had been to hold the Ebro line in Spain after the elder Scipios' disaster. Still more remarkably, his colleague Livius Salinator, facing the new Punic invasion, had held no command at all during the war to date. Even stranger, the two men were old enemies. Yet, prompted by veteran leaders such as Fabius Maximus, this was the pair deliberately elected to the consulship for the crisis. Like the surprise selection of the youthful Scipio for Spain three years before, the choice of this odd couple paid off.

On learning that Hasdrubal was marching from the Po valley southwards, Nero selected the best 6,000 foot and 1,000 horse from his own army and led them north by forced marches to link up with

Livius. The rest of his army was left under subordinates, who proved fully able to hold Hannibal's attention. When in turn Hasdrubal realised, near Fanum (Fano) on the Adriatic coast, that he was facing both consuls, he assumed that his brother had suffered a catastrophic defeat. He put his own army into hasty retreat, only to be caught and crushed by the river Metaurus – Nero's troops inflicting the decisive flank assault. Rather than trying to save something from the wreck, the middle Barcid brother rode into the Roman ranks for a glorious death. The date was 22 June, ten years and a day since Hannibal's triumph at Lake Trasimene.

Hannibal was told of the disaster in a famous and grisly Roman gesture. Nero brought back Hasdrubal's head to Apulia a few days later.

> He ordered it to be tossed before the forward posts of the enemy. He also had his African prisoners put on display for the enemy, wearing their chains, and two he released, telling them to go to Hannibal and recount to him what had taken place. Shaken by this great blow to his people as well as his family, Hannibal is said to have stated that he now saw clearly the destiny of Carthage.[27]

The entire character of the war had changed. He evacuated everyone from Metapontum and from still-faithful Lucanian towns, and transferred them and his army into Bruttium. In 206 all of Lucania submitted to the Romans.

Hannibal at bay

Bruttium became the final redoubt of Carthaginian power for the next three years, the last defiant remnant of the great expedition. From now on Hannibal husbanded his resources. Reportedly he had trouble obtaining enough supplies locally, while in 205 a large supply-fleet from Carthage fell into enemy hands and an epidemic struck both the Punic and the Roman armies. Roman commanders as usual avoided pitched battles and preferred skirmishing harassments. Hannibal in turn made no attempt to recover lost ground, only to hold what he still had. Even this was gradually cut back, Locri falling to the Romans in 205 and northern parts of Bruttium defecting the year after.

It is hard to be sure why Hannibal hung on when south Italy was an obvious lost cause. There was nothing to be hoped for from Philip V of Macedon, whose involvement had dropped to nothing years earlier and who in 205 made peace with the Romans. By contrast, elsewhere the Carthaginians themselves still fought hard. In Spain, where Hasdrubal son of Gisco had taken over command and Mago, the youngest Barcid, was his deputy, Scipio made little progress in 207. The two generals were able to rebuild their forces to massive size – 74,000 men according to Polybius, or a more conservative 54,500 in Livy – by the time he again advanced into the south in spring 206. In the battle of Ilipa they were nevertheless routed by superior generalship, but it took months more to end Carthaginian resistance, for Mago continued full of fight though his colleague sailed for home. Even when finally expelled from Spain, Mago moved to the Balearic islands (today's Mahón in Minorca supposedly commemorates him) and in 205, strongly reinforced from Carthage, landed on the Ligurian coast of Italy itself. Fresh forces were sent by sea to him there, including a few elephants, to give him no fewer than 21,000 men, including 2,000 cavalry, along with lavish funds for raising Ligurian and Gallic troops. His instructions were to try, once more, to link up with Hannibal.

This vigorous activity must have been known to Hannibal and, indeed, was probably authorised by him. It is true that now Hasdrubal son of Gisco seems to have been the dominant personality at Carthage. Livy so describes him, and in 205 he made his daughter

Sophoniba a queen by marrying her to the victorious Syphax, who had now conquered eastern Numidia with Carthage's blessing – thus making an exile and enemy of Masinissa. He also took charge of the defence of Punic Africa when the Roman invasion came the following year. After so many setbacks in recent years, from the fall of Syracuse and Capua to the Metaurus, it should be no surprise to find that the Barcids' previous supremacy in the republic had been weakened, even to the point where at home an independently strong ally such as Hasdrubal son of Gisco enjoyed effective primacy.

But Hasdrubal had the disaster of Ilipa and the loss of Spain to his own discredit. His faction and that of the Barcids needed each other. Nothing suggests, in fact, that he saw himself as a rival to Hannibal or was unsympathetic to him. Mago's continuation in command and the efforts from home to support his brother – the Ligurian expedition and the supply-fleet intercepted by the Romans – show that the son of Gisco and the Barcids remained collaborators in prosecuting the war.

Other questions arise all the same. To start with, why was Mago sent to the Italian Riviera with a mission to join forces with Hannibal, who was over 600 miles away at the other end of the peninsula? The brothers were actually closer to Carthage than to each other – and Hannibal's military situation by 205 was much worse than in 207, when their brother's invasion had met with destruction. And if joining Hannibal was not the aim of Mago's expedition, the venture was even more predictably futile. Instead of his operating with numerous troops and copious funds in Liguria, it would have been more productive to try to land in Bruttium with them. Nor was that self-evidently impossible, for Roman fleets could be eluded as the Ligurian landing itself shows, and as Hannibal in turn was to do two years later.

Again, we might ask why Hannibal did not evacuate his Bruttian redoubt now, either to join his brother or – more valuably – to go to Africa and lead its defence against invasion. Everyone knew that invasion was looming: Scipio, consul in 205, went to Sicily to organise the veterans of Cannae into an expeditionary army. There were still plentiful military resources available to Carthage, as the first years of the invasion would show, not to mention the forces which Syphax contributed; meanwhile, leaving defence in the hands of Hasdrubal son of Gisco was to prove a recipe for fresh disasters. In Bruttium meanwhile, year after year, Hannibal himself faced mounting frustrations. From his redoubt he could do little to obstruct Scipio's invasion preparations – or at any rate he made little attempt to, with his army short of food and hit by plague.

In 205 he failed to prevent Locri from defecting as well. Too late, he marched on the town, to be boldly confronted by outnumbered Roman forces under none other than Scipio, who had arrived from Sicily. Hannibal promptly retired from the area – possibly one of history's great missed opportunities. Had he overwhelmed Scipio, he might yet have saved Africa and Carthage. His only other significant activity was to write the famous record of his achievements, in Punic and Greek, and set it up in Hera's temple at Cape Lacinium, where it remained for Polybius to read forty years later. This very act conceded that the grand expedition to Italy was now effectively dead.

All this raises a third question: how did Hannibal view Carthage's war situation at this stage? There was no prospect now of imposing victorious terms. The only realistic hope was a compromise peace, something he would still propose three years later to Scipio: and in 205 or 204 Carthage would have had a better hand to play, with troops – 40–50,000 in all even now – on two Italian fronts, her own territories in Africa still intact, and her ally Syphax in control of all Numidia. Now might have been the time to send Hanno or Mago the Samnite (or a high-ranking prisoner such as Cincius) to sound out the Romans on ending hostilities. We can be certain that this never happened: Roman historians would have taken delight in reporting how their countrymen spurned any such offer just as they had spurned his approaches after Cannae. Perhaps Hannibal, and at Carthage Hasdrubal son of Gisco, knew that overtures would be rejected; perhaps they simply hoped that something might yet happen – a shattering victory by Mago in the north, for instance – to tilt the table in Carthage's favour. While they waited, Scipio invaded.

Scipio invades Africa

During 204 the expeditionary army landed near Utica. Its core was the pair of legions originally formed twelve years earlier from the survivors of Cannae, who had served with distinction – but without release – in Sicily ever since. No doubt they looked forward to their revenge. Yet the entire army totalled hardly more than 30,000 troops, including cavalry, and its escort fleet was small, a mere 40 warships. Hasdrubal son of Gisco could have organised forces of equal, or larger, size ready to confront the invasion; instead, it was only after the Roman landing that he levied troops. The units that Hannibal had sent in 218 to defend Punic Africa had no doubt been sent elsewhere by now, but nothing had replaced them – even though the Romans had resumed naval raiding on the coasts every year from 207 on.

Scipio besieged Utica for a while, got nowhere and then, encamped on the coast nearby with winter approaching, was faced by strong Punic and Numidian armies. Hasdrubal had won the support of Syphax, partly by backing him in his conquest of eastern Numidia, and partly by giving him in marriage his own beautiful and accomplished daughter Sophoniba (the 'Sophonisba' of eighteenth-century tragedies: her Punic name was Safonba'al). Scipio in turn was joined by the ousted claimant to that kingdom, Masinissa,

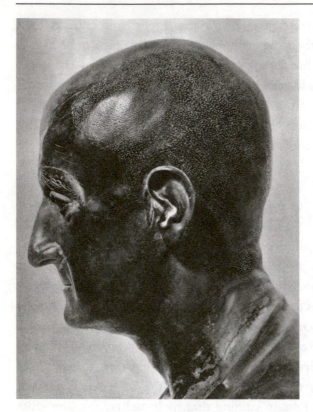

Bronze bust in
Naples, sometimes
identified as Scipio
(an alternative
suggestion is
a priest of the
Egyptian goddess
Isis).

who had understandably small forces. In the circumstances, the
Carthaginian response to the invasion was peculiarly lethargic. By
land the two armies, Punic and Numidian, blockaded the Romans
in their beachhead; at sea the Punic navy – which as recently as
208 had a hundred or more ships in commission – kept clear of the
scene.

Hannibal could do nothing about this. He may well have started to
plan how and when to evacuate Italy, but it had to be done with care,
for Roman fleets patrolled Italian and Sicilian waters. Meanwhile in
Bruttium the usual skirmishes with the enemy, marching clashes,
withdrawals and regroupings continued during 204 and into 203.

Not only did such actions do him little good, but he may have known by now the Romans actually wanted to keep him in south Italy and Mago in the far north. It was the final triumph of Fabius' and Marcellus' methods of war: they had rendered the Barcid brothers irrelevant to the critical theatre of operations.

As 203 opened, his city's fortunes collapsed. Scipio disarmed his opponents' suspicions by negotiating for a compromise peace, an outcome that appealed to both the son of Gisco and Syphax. Hasdrubal expected, perhaps, that achieving peace would give him and his circle lasting dominance at Carthage, forcing the discredited Barcid faction to join his or be sidelined. For Syphax, it would buttress his rule over a united Numidia. Once their alertness slackened, Scipio broke off talks, set fire to their camps in the dead of night, and slaughtered their scattering troops. Though Hasdrubal and Syphax escaped inland, rallied survivors and raised fresh levies, they were pursued and totally routed in another Scipionic triumph on the Great Plains near Bulla Regia. When Scipio marched back to the coast and occupied Tunes just outside Carthage, the Punic senate asked for a truce and for terms.

Hannibal was surely kept informed of events, for the authorities at Carthage had no trouble contacting him when they wanted him to return (just as they had had little or none keeping in touch with him since 216), nor had he any in transporting his veterans to Africa afterwards. When he did return, he was automatically supreme commander there, confirming that any decisions about peace needed to involve him from the start. Meanwhile the Carthaginians at home – in practice The Mighty Ones (the senate) and, we may infer, the sufetes – worked out peace terms with Scipio, which were then taken to Rome by his trusted lieutenant Laelius for ratification.

These terms recalled Hannibal and Mago from Italy (as was to be expected), left the Punic republic intact in Africa but took away the Spanish province created by the Barcids, imposed a war-indemnity,

Masinissa, King of Numidia, Probably a fanciful sculptured head of Carthage's successful rival and ultimate nemesis, in Rome.

and (symbolically the most wounding detail) reduced the navy to 20 ships – one-tenth its theoretical wartime strength. Scipio was making it clear to Carthage and Hannibal that there would be no more overseas ventures. There were to be few or none even in Africa, for he recognised Masinissa as king of all Numidia in place of the overthrown and captured Syphax.

Hannibal's return

What followed remains debated. Polybius' narrative of events is only partly preserved, but it quite plainly has the terms being ratified at Rome and word reaching both Scipio and Carthage some while later. This must have been late in 203, before sailing stopped for the winter. Even before this, Hannibal and Mago had received their recall messages: for Hannibal was already back in Africa before the sailing season ended. With him came his army, by now (it seems) largely south Italian in strength. Mago's army afterwards arrived too, though by then Mago himself was dead of a wound suffered in a last defeat in north Italy. After Hannibal's landing at Leptis Minor, in the Emporia region on the Gulf of Sirte (modern Lamta near Sousse), a Roman supply convoy was blown off course onto the shore near Carthage and was thoroughly plundered. Then Scipio's envoys, sent in a warship to the city to protest, were attacked on the return trip by ships sent out by pro-war Carthaginians. Thereupon the Roman general denounced the truce, declared the peace a dead letter, and began to ravage the surrounding countryside. Hannibal stayed in Emporia, rebuilding his army.

This sequence of events prompts various questions. The most extraordinary detail, but perhaps the least important, is Livy's claim that the Senate rejected Scipio's peace terms when Carthaginian envoys came to Rome to ratify them – not on the ground that the terms were too mild, but because the envoys were arrogant and could not be trusted. His account is quite unconvincing, for not only does he manage to avoid admitting that the terms were Scipio's but he tries to depict Scipio's closest friend and aide, Laelius, as opposing the very agreement that his friend had just fashioned. Yet Livy then treats the renewal of the war as entirely the Carthaginians' fault, and reports alarm at Rome at the return to hostilities. The alleged rejection looks like a clumsy and unprepossessing error.

More striking is Hannibal's easy return to his homeland, not by himself but together with thousands of troops. Some others had been left to garrison the last remaining allied towns (no doubt they soon capitulated), while later Roman propaganda alleged a massacre of thousands of Bruttians when they refused to accompany him. This is not to be believed, for the soldiers whom he led to Africa were mostly Bruttian, with perhaps some other still loyal Italians. Not many of the fabled conquerors of the Alps can have remained after fifteen years' campaigning. The consuls in Bruttium had been under orders to keep him there and Roman warships watched the coasts – yet, without interference, Hannibal acquired or even built a transport fleet which must have numbered several hundred; had a Punic naval escort rendezvous with these on the Bruttian coast; and reached Leptis Minor without incident – though (in Livy's rather overdrawn picture) with nearly as much heartache as if he were leaving his native land. Roman surveillance by both land and sea had plainly become lax; in fact the consuls were reprimanded for letting him get away.

Even so his evacuation of the army was a remarkable feat. Preparations must have taken months: a clue that, well before Scipio's peace terms had been accepted at Carthage, perhaps after the burning of the camps, Hannibal had started planning his long-deferred – and, indeed, unwisely deferred – departure. His heartache on leaving we can believe, for other reasons than Livy's. The grand expedition had come to nothing after so many years; most of the faithful 26,000 of the Alpine march were gone, as were his brothers, and we no longer hear of Hanno his nephew, the cavalryman Maharbal, or Hannibal the Gladiator. Instead of imposing Carthaginian hegemony over the western Mediterranean, now he would be in the position that he had forced on the enemy for so many years – shielding his homeland from the ravages of invaders. He may well have acknowledged, though not enjoyed, the irony.

This leads to a crucial question: on what basis did he return? He would expect the peace terms to include the evacuation of Italy by all Punic forces. The obvious corollary was that these must then be disbanded or, at least, placed under Scipio's orders. This was not done, if our sources tell the story even roughly right. Hannibal kept his troops in Emporia, added Mago's survivors to them, levied local recruits, and cast about for fresh Numidian cavalry (not an easy task with Masinissa imposing his control over the kingdom). In a curious and contradictory way, the ancient sources treat him almost as an entity separate from the Punic state and the peace terms – as though these did not affect, or were not recognised by, Carthage's chief general even on his return.

Scipio's own calculations deserve query too. According to Livy, his lieutenant Laelius told the Senate that 'Scipio had premised his hopes of a peace accord on the expectation that Hannibal and Mago would not be recalled from Italy'.[28] Livy's attempt to make Laelius look like an opponent of the peace can be discounted, as we saw, but this item can be believed. It was obviously not desirable to have the Barcid brothers bring their armies over to Africa before peace was ratified. Once it was ratified, on the other hand, their sole legitimate option would be to come home and there disband their men.

But Hannibal arrived in Africa before the news of ratification did, and this seems to have rekindled pro-war feeling at Carthage. What followed, as our sources tell it, was the plundering of the Roman supply-fleet and the attack on Scipio's envoys. Scipio in turn declared the truce broken, and that war would resume.

The campaign of Zama

Clearly the whole negotiations episode was marked by suspicion on both sides, so it is not surprising that the upshot was fresh hostilities. More surprising is that Scipio was at least as ready as

Hannibal for these. Hannibal, on home ground (if for the first time since childhood) and with Carthage still untouched, could now – if he chose – apply Fabian tactics, in his turn, to wear down the invaders. Scipio had a relatively small army on foreign soil, was receiving no reinforcements, and a severe defeat would be as disastrous for him as it had been in 255 for the earlier Roman invasion. Yet he made no effort to learn whether the peace, now ratified at Rome, would still be honoured at Carthage despite the outrages. Nor, it seems, did he try to ascertain whether Hannibal would abide by it. We must infer that Scipio treated Hannibal's armed return, and armed buildup in Emporia, as a *de facto* rejection of peace, even if he then alleged other reasons for renewing hostilities against Carthage. Plainly he was confident of victory, even in a battle with the victor of Cannae.

The Romans moved into the countryside to ravage and plunder, no doubt with the aim of provoking Hannibal to battle before he could build a larger army. Scipio's military situation was now uncannily like Hannibal's in late 217: two great victories, the invader looting and destroying where he pleased, but no defections to him by allied towns or peoples, and his army at risk of eroding. What saved him was that the Carthaginian state no longer had manpower resources equal to those of Rome in 217 – or even those it had itself deployed as recently as 207 – and that Hannibal, perhaps for that same reason, did not opt to follow him and harass his movements.

The course of events is blurred, all the same. Scipio marched across the countryside, most likely through the fertile and populous Bagradas region, sacking towns and plundering the land. The ancient accounts would imply no more than a few weeks or months between him resuming hostilities and Hannibal confronting him at the misnamed battle of Zama. In reality, items of evidence suggest that it was about a year, from the supply-fleet episode in late 203 until Zama in October 202; and even if the fleet episode dates instead to early 202, the gap is still six to seven months. For, according to the later historian Dio, an eclipse of the sun occurred as Zama was being fought. Such an eclipse did occur in October: it was hardly visible in North Africa and is not mentioned by Polybius or Livy, so Dio's item on its own might not carry weight. But Livy records a final battle – the defeat of Syphax's son, bringing Numidian reinforcements for Hannibal after missing Zama – as dating to 17 December by the Roman calendar, and he indicates that this was not long after Zama: indeed, by the erratic Roman calendar the real date may even have been in November. Finally, Scipio's new and harsher terms were promptly agreed to at Carthage, with Hannibal's own support, and were ratified at Rome in early 201, which makes dating Zama to the first half of 202 less plausible.

Scipio thus had all spring and summer 202 to treat the countryside of Punic Africa as mercilessly as Hannibal had treated the countryside of Italy. To deal with the plunder and keep his troops ready for possible battle, he probably marched repeatedly from his base outside Utica into the countryside, bringing fire and the sword to different areas, then returning to base to store the booty and prepare the next raid. Apart from Hannibal's army over in Emporia, there were no Carthaginian forces to stop him. It is understandable that the city authorities sent message after message imploring their general to act.

Who was in charge in the city at this date is unknown. Hanno the Great (still alive) and his group had just as minimal a say in affairs, even now, as over the past three and a half decades. Hasdrubal son of Gisco had lost popularity and political standing, thanks to his relentless capacity to suffer defeats at Scipio's hands; and, in one later account, he was now driven to suicide by his fellow citizens' hostility. At all events he disappears from the record. Still, as events were showing, the bulk of the Carthaginian people – and their leaders – remained full of fight. Most of the magistrates and much of the senate, therefore, still supported the Barcid faction or what remained of Hasdrubal's faction, for both were still pugnacious. In fact, with the son of Gisco gone, his supporters may well have gravitated to the Barcids, to restore Barcid supremacy at home for one last spell. The Carthaginians certainly had no qualms at the renewal of hostilities. They urged Hannibal to confront Scipio and destroy him as soon as possible. Hannibal's reply was tersely military: he would march when he was ready, and not before.

As the year 202 wore on, Scipio moved further west, nearer to Numidia, for with Hannibal's forces growing he, in turn, needed reinforcements from Masinissa of both cavalry and infantry. The new king was busy bringing the rest of Numidia under his rule, and took his time. This left Scipio in an extraordinarily dangerous position, over a hundred miles inland from his bridgehead near Utica, leading 23,000 foot and only 1,500 horse, in the midst of a ravaged and enraged countryside. Had Hannibal chosen to follow and harass him with tactics like those of Marcellus (or like those of the 'truceless' rebels who had confronted Hamilcar in Punic Africa itself, thirty-five years before), the results could well have favoured the home forces. Hannibal might have worn the Roman army down and cut it off from Masinissa's aid, thereby sending a signal, too, to that wily king – whose own family ties to the Barcids went back four decades – to rethink his allegiances.

Scipio did not even have to be confronted in a risky battle. He could not afford damagingly prolonged campaigning, either in military or in political terms, for, if confined to desultory and wasting warfare, he definitely risked being replaced. At Rome, self-confident consuls in 203 and 202 (and even later, in 201) kept trying to take over the military command in Africa. Quite likely Hannibal heard of these consular attempts, for they were public and there was plenty of time for word to reach Africa. Any replacement, of course, was certain to be outgeneralled by him. One way or another, there was still the chance of some kind of compromise peace: the Romans had reduced their overall armed forces substantially, and already were looking with suspicion at Philip V's doings across the Adriatic. There was much to be said, then, for using Fabian attrition against Scipio.

But Hannibal had never been a general in the Fabian mould by choice. Perhaps, too, memories of Carthage's long and terrible 'Truceless' War, when much of Punic Africa was laid waste, pushed him to seek a faster outcome. He adopted the Romans' programme before Cannae: to build up as large an army as possible to crush the invaders in battle. He equipped it with a strong elephant corps, more than eighty in all – over twice as many as in the battle by the Tagus in 220 or at the Trebia in 218 – and eventually was joined by another kinsman of the fallen Syphax who brought in 2,000 valuable Numidian horsemen. It was only after this, in early autumn 202, that he set out from Hadrumetum in Emporia with about 40,000 infantry and 4,000 cavalry to find Scipio.

His march went by Zama, one of several towns so named in the hinterland: probably the one later called Zama Regia (today a site called Seba Biar, fifteen miles south-east of Le Kef). Zama, though only an encampment on the march, gave its name to the battle through a careless mistake by his biographer Nepos two centuries later. Everything was on a knife-edge. Scipio still had not been reinforced by Masinissa and so was heavily outnumbered, especially in cavalry. Hannibal's veterans from Italy were 15–20,000 strong, if Polybius is right that they were about equal to Scipio's entire Roman infantry. The rest of the troops, however, were foreign mercenaries, including the Ligurian and Gallic survivors of Mago's army, and recent Carthaginian and African levies. That may be why his movements in this, his last campaign and his only one in Africa, were curiously deliberate, beginning with the long stay in Emporia. Now he chose neither to manoeuvre skilfully – for example to get west of Scipio and block Numidian reinforcements – nor to press an immediate attack, but instead arranged a meeting, under truce, with his opponent.

Scipio encamped near a place which Polybius calls Margaron and Livy Naraggara (the Greek name looks like a version of the Latin) – and, crucially, Masinissa had now arrived with 6,000 foot and 4,000 horse. In Roman times Naraggara stood in the hilly and scenic region twenty-five miles by road west of Sicca, probably at or near today's Sakiet Sidi Youssef on the Tunisian–Algerian border. Hannibal moved to pitch camp on a waterless hill a few miles away to the east. Whether or not he knew that Masinissa had come in, the die was cast for battle. Nearby lay level ground: the most widely held view is that it was the plain some miles south or south-east of Sicca (about 16 miles south-east of Sakiet Sidi Youssef and not far from Le Kef's airport today). First, however – on 18 October if the battle was fought on the 19th – the two men met, each with an interpreter although both could speak Greek.

Some modern scholars doubt that this famous rendezvous took place, holding that a personal meeting between the two greatest commanders of the day is too obviously dramatic. Yet hardly any other pair of great generals is recorded as conferring before they clashed in battle (not Alexander with his Persian opponent, for instance, or Caesar with Pompey, Richard I with Saladin, or Napoleon with Wellington), nor is it even a regular theme of battle-stories about obscurer leaders. Polybius probably and Livy certainly embroider what was said, but with Silenus and Sosylus able to record Hannibal's side of the interview, and Laelius (whom Polybius later knew) back with Scipio, the gist of the conversation in Polybius should be trusted.

Hannibal offered advice and a peace that conceded all disputed overseas territories to the Romans:

All that there remains for us to do is to try our best to deprecate the wrath of the gods, and to put an end, as far as in us lies, to these feelings of obstinate hostility. ... I am that Hannibal who, after the battle of Cannae, became master of nearly all Italy ... but now I am in Libya debating with you, a Roman, as to the bare existence of myself and my countrymen. ... What man of sense would deliberately choose to incur the risk which is now before you? If you conquer, you will add nothing of importance to your glory or that of your country; while, if you are worsted, you will have been yourself the means of entirely cancelling all the honours and glories you have already won. ... [My point] is that the Romans should retain all the countries for which we have hitherto contended, ... and that the Carthaginians should engage never to go to war with Rome for these; and also that the islands lying between Italy and Libya should belong to Rome. For I am persuaded that such a treaty will be at once safest for the Carthaginians, and most glorious for you and the entire people of Rome.

Scipio had imposed virtually the same territorial losses the year before, while Hannibal said nothing about an indemnity or the virtual dismantling of the Punic navy, both of which had also figured in Scipio's terms. What is striking is that, in the peace which followed, Carthage did give up her overseas territories (even Ebusus) and undertook not to make war outside Africa – simply a stricter form of the proviso that Hannibal proposed to Scipio. Similarly, the other peace-provisos would be largely tightened up from those of 203. This does raise the question of why there was a battle at all, and tens of thousands of lives lost.

Scipio's reply may hint at the answer. He emphasised that Hannibal had been forced out of Italy and Punic Africa was now under Roman control:

Your countrymen have been beaten, and at their earnest prayer we arranged a written treaty, in which, besides the offer now made by you, it was provided that the Carthaginians should restore prisoners without ransom, should surrender all their decked vessels, pay five thousand talents, and give hostages for their performance of these articles. ... The Senate agreed: the people ratified the treaty. ... What course is left to me? Put yourself in my place and say. To withdraw the severest clauses of the treaty? ... If a still severer clause were added to the conditions imposed, it might be possible to refer the treaty back to the people; but, if I were to withdraw any of these conditions, such a reference does not admit even of discussion. What then is the conclusion of my discourse? It is, that you must submit yourselves and your country to us unconditionally, or conquer us in the field.[29]

Deliberately or mistakenly, he interpreted Hannibal's proposals as the only ones that Carthage was prepared to discuss. Hannibal had perhaps reckoned that non-territorial provisos could be worked out later, since he could not seriously expect Scipio to drop them all. The point could have been cleared up in less than a hour's discussion – but Scipio had not accepted the rendezvous to negotiate. His attitude was that of the Romans down many generations: there would be no conclusion, harsh or benign, without the other side being uncontestably defeated and admitting defeat.

Hannibal had probably expected this. The proposals he was putting to Scipio would have been the only realistic ones that Carthage could offer Rome even if the invader now went down to destruction. He may have felt it a duty to test the dubious chance that Scipio himself might accept such a compromise, to earn the renown of ending the war and avert any fresh efforts to take away his command on the brink of victory. To offer a simple capitulation was impossible, with his army still in being and his city relying on him. In any case,

Hannibal wanted to meet the young man whose military genius was equal to his own, who had overthrown his family's and country's rule in Spain, reduced Punic power to the walls of Carthage and the circuit of Hannibal's own camp, and who by the end of the following day might be dead – or be master of Africa.

The battle of Zama – as it may still be traditionally called – next day was another curiously deliberate affair. Like Napoleon at Waterloo, Hannibal had no inspired manoeuvre or surprise attack in store but settled for what was essentially a head-to-head struggle. His army, like Scipio's, stood in three infantry lines with cavalry on their flanks and the elephants in front: Mago's men and the mercenaries formed a first line 12,000 strong, the Carthaginian and Libyan recruits the second, and his own army from Italy the third. First of all, the 80-odd elephants charged at the enemy. But whatever Hannibal expected of them, he was disappointed. Scipio's light-armed troops, most of them veterans like the rest of his army, drove the animals off despite suffering casualties – and in fact some of the harassed animals veered to throw into confusion first one Punic cavalry wing and then the other.

Masinissa and Laelius, facing the wings with the Numidian and Roman horse, promptly charged to exploit the situation, pursuing the Punic horse into the distance, and thus depriving Hannibal of his entire mounted arm almost from the outset. It is not plausible that he intentionally sacrificed his horsemen, including the long-awaited Numidians, so as to deprive Scipio of his in turn. Operating without cavalry was a novel tactical situation for him, unlike his opponent.

Meanwhile his three infantry lines waited to receive the enemy's. This was Hannibal's normal battle-posture – only at Trasimene had he himself made the first infantry attack – but the loss of cavalry had never happened before. The infantry battle proceeded at a deliberate pace, almost in slow motion, and in phases largely separate from one another. First, the Punic first line was forced back and then broken by its Roman equivalent; then the second-line Carthaginians and Libyans battled the oncoming Romans – perhaps Scipio's first and second lines together. Not only did the two Punic lines fail to support each other similarly, but the Carthaginians and Libyans (presumably following orders) refused to admit their retreating front-line comrades into their ranks. In fact, they came to serious blows with them to drive them off, even as the Romans bore down on them all. Then the second line in its turn was broken and scattered.

While all this was going on, Hannibal and his veterans of Italy watched. He made no move to take advantage of the Romans' furious engagement with his first two lines – not even to try to rally one or other of the collapsing contingents. Indeed, when men from the second shattered line streamed back towards his remaining corps, they were forced aside just as they had forced away the front-liners. He was perhaps expecting – or rather gambling – that these first stages of fighting would damage the Romans badly enough to enable his veterans to deliver a *coup de grâce*. But Scipio's third-line troops, the *triarii*, toughest in a legionary array though the fewest, were still not engaged. They perhaps even deterred Hannibal from any forward move after the rest of his army was swept from the field: for, still without interference from him, Scipio's men now paused, removed their wounded and rearranged their ranks into a single, much longer line – Roman legionaries and Italian allies – before advancing on the veterans. Many in that long array, as Hannibal surely knew, were the legionaries who had survived Cannae.

With troops on both sides similarly armed, similarly experienced and, indeed, similarly Italian, this third stage was fought with concentrated fury. A civil-war battle between Roman armies a century and a half later, vividly described by Appian from a contemporary account, could fit exactly:

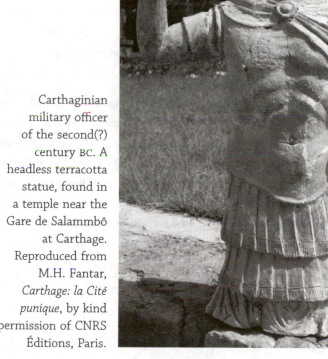

Carthaginian military officer of the second(?) century BC. A headless terracotta statue, found in a temple near the Gare de Salammbô at Carthage. Reproduced from M.H. Fantar, *Carthage: la Cité punique*, by kind permission of CNRS Éditions, Paris.

Thus urged on rather by their own animosity and ambition than by their generals they assailed each other, considering this their own affair. Being veterans they raised no battle-cry, since they could not expect to terrify each other, nor in the engagement did they utter a sound, either as victors or vanquished. ... They stood together in close order, and since neither could dislodge the other they locked together with their swords as in a wrestling match. No blow missed its mark. There were wounds and slaughter but no cries, only groans; and when one fell he was instantly borne away and another took his place. They needed neither admonition nor encouragement, since experience had made each one his own general. When they were overcome by fatigue they drew apart from each other for a brief space to take breath, as in gymnastic games, and then rushed again to the encounter. Amazement took possession of [observers], as they beheld such deeds done with such precision and in such silence.[30]

We are not told what had become of the remains of the first two Carthaginian lines (not to mention the surviving elephants), or of the Roman light-armed troops or even Masinissa's Numidian foot-soldiers. Obviously they played no part in this grinding infantry struggle, unless some of the beaten Punic soldiers regrouped alongside the veterans from Italy; but, just as likely or more so, the Roman light-armed and the Numidian foot kept them all on the run from the field. Yet the prospects for victory still favoured Hannibal, though barely so. His veterans were not much (if at all) fewer than Scipio's 20,000 infantry, according to Polybius, and they had done no fighting yet.

Hannibal's own rôle was, it seems, as static as his army's. Who his chief officers were is not known but, even if some from the old days were still with him – his nephew Hanno, for instance, or old Maharbal, or his friends Mago and Hannibal – they showed as little dash as he did. After an optimistic speech to his own veterans before the battle, he simply stayed with them while the opening rounds were left to the unnamed commanders of the two forward lines. When his veterans in turn closed with the enemy, he may have joined in the fighting, but even this is not recorded (unless we incautiously believe Appian's fancy that the two generals clashed in an inconclusive duel – followed by one between Hannibal and a suddenly present Masinissa). Nor did he seek to guard his flanks or

Polybius, a plaster cast of a relief portrait set up at Cleitor in Arcadia by a descendant in the third century AD; the original remains in Greece, reportedly in a deteriorating state. Polybius is dressed as a soldier, with lance and sword, and with a shield and helmet on the ground behind him. The cast is held by the Archäologisches Institut, Universität Freiburg-im-Bremen, and the illustration is reproduced with its kind permission.

rear against possible threat; perhaps it was impossible once he had lost his cavalry, elephants and the bulk of his infantry. The outcome was all but predictable. With the veterans of Italy bloodily pinned down in front by the men of Cannae, Masinissa and Laelius brought their cavalry back from the pursuit to take Hannibal in the rear.

As his army collapsed, Hannibal rode off the field almost alone. Two days later he reached Hadrumetum, a sustained gallop of 120 miles. He left behind his own Cannae, with nearly half his men dead – Polybius says 20,000 – and almost as many captured, as against total Roman losses of under two thousand.

In Polybius' view, 'he had done in the battle all that was to be
expected of a good and experienced general': using elephants to break
the enemy's front, buttressing the veterans' line with the expendable
first and second lines so as to blunt the Romans' advance, and
keeping his best corps fresh until needed. This judgement, which no
doubt Silenus and Sosylus had pronounced too, is widely accepted.
Yet it is not easy to see the genius of the Tagus, Trebia, Trasimene
and Cannae at work at Zama or, indeed, throughout the campaign.
To blame the poor quality of Mago's men and the local recruits is
no solution, for Hannibal had had the best part of a year to train
them and, in fact, had refused to pursue Scipio until he judged them
ready. He miscalculated equally in putting off confrontation as long
as he did, for his delay allowed Masinissa to reinforce the Romans,
and it was their resulting superiority in cavalry – for the first time
in his battles – that would prove decisive. Then, when he finally did
move, his insistence on an immediate pitched battle, rather than a
slower outcome by manoeuvre and attrition, was questionable (all
the more so if over half the army was in fact poor in quality).

On the day, it is noteworthy how none of the measures that
Polybius praises actually worked. His elephants did not shatter
the Roman front, his first and second lines failed to blunt the
enemy's advance, the freshness of his third line was countered by
the freshness of at any rate Scipio's *triarii*, nor was it exploited by
any earlier manoeuvres – like when much of the Roman infantry
was locked in combat and a blow from the most practised veterans
in the world might have decided everything. Instead, Hannibal's
compartmentalised handling of his disparate lines, none supporting
another, was a striking contrast to how he had once used equally
varied contingents – most effectively at Cannae.

For Hannibal and Carthage, Zama was a disaster worse than
Cannae. It is clear that he was outgeneralled by Scipio, whose forces
had attained combat skills rare even for Romans. Scipio's first line,

perhaps with help from the second though none is mentioned, bore the brunt of both opening stages of the battle; then the Roman troops obeyed the trumpet-calls to step back and realign their ranks – without interference – before closing with the Punic third line. Again, unlike Hannibal's anonymous and unimpressive lieutenants, Scipio was seconded by two able cavalrymen, Masinissa and Laelius, whose control over their squadrons – as firm as Scipio's over the infantry – made victory certain.

Even if Hannibal had done all that a good general could on the battlefield, his hurried flight from it must have dismayed the survivors in his army. Like Napoleon after Waterloo, he abandoned them to their own devices. What prompted him can only be surmised: the army's near-total destruction, fear of being captured by vengeful enemies and transported for display at Rome (like Syphax recently) or – in some charitable interpretations – a belief that he should not risk himself when he still had much to offer his country. Even this cold-blooded calculation, though, need not have prevented him from trying to rally what was left of the men who had followed him from Italy or joined him locally with trust in his leadership. The flight from the field of disaster suggests that, for a spell, his spirit simply collapsed.

But by the time he went on to Carthage from Hadrumetum, his first entry into his home city since the age of nine, he had recovered himself and was ready to fight one more battle – this time for peace.

CHAPTER 7

HANNIBAL IN POLITICS
(201–195)

The peace of 201

Even now resistance could have gone on (another parallel with Napoleon in 1815). At Hadrumetum, where Hannibal probably had left a garrison, he managed to rally 6,500 horse and foot, according to Appian, and there must still have been some troops garrisoning Carthage, just as there were still warships and crews in its ports. Even though the authorities soon sent Scipio a new peace-delegation, many Carthaginians wanted to fight on. A revealing incident took place soon after Hannibal himself entered the city and Scipio's new terms were brought back.

> [A senator] Gisco came forward to speak against settlement, and he was receiving a hearing from the crowd ... Hannibal grabbed Gisco with his hand, and pulled him down from the raised dais. The sight of this, unfamiliar in a free community, provoked a buzz of disapproval amongst the people[31]

– clearly not just at the rudeness of Hannibal's act but because the senator he silenced was advocating continued war. This is the latest of many items of evidence showing that the Barcids, far from having imposed a self-interested war on their unwilling fellow citizens, had been in tune, until now, with strongly held sentiment at home. Yet further resistance would have been ultimately hopeless. For all that Hannibal and his fellow citizens knew, Zama might bring enough reinforcements to Scipio for him to starve out Carthage itself. By contrast, to accept his new terms promptly would preserve her North African territories, and quite possibly avert violent upheavals within a dying and embittered city.

Sentiment turned in Hannibal's favour again once he explained the situation. Moreover (as noted earlier) Scipio's new terms were not a radical contrast to those of the previous year, though harsher and with some additions. Harsher demands were inevitable but, on the other hand, Scipio had no wish to lay siege to Carthage's mighty fortifications, or risk being superseded – even now – by a consul ambitious for the glory of dictating peace. He still imposed no territorial losses in Africa, but the Punic indemnity was doubled to 10,000 talents over fifty years, the permissible number of warships halved to 10 triremes, and war-elephants forbidden. Forbidden, too, was war by Carthage outside Africa; within Africa it would require Roman approval. This and the ban on war-elephants obviously precluded any future territorial expansion. Less noted at the time, but pregnant with future trouble, was a new clause requiring that Masinissa should recover from Carthage all lands and property which he or his ancestors had possessed – an indefinite proviso that the king would soon start to exploit.

The Romans made no demand for Hannibal to be handed over to them or otherwise punished, though they had called for precisely this in 218. Just recently, Scipio had been eager to seize not only the defeated Syphax as a war-trophy but also his Carthaginian queen Sophoniba, who killed herself to avoid it. The restraint over Hannibal contrasts, too, with the hounding to which the Romans would subject him later. It must have been thanks to Scipio, who genuinely admired his adversary and was to oppose future persecution of him.

Once the peace was ratified at Rome early in 201, Scipio dramatised the end of hostilities, and of Carthage as a major power, by having all but the permitted ten of the republic's war vessels towed into deep water – some 500 of all types – and burnt in sight of the city. This symbolically marked the end, too, of the Barcids' supremacy in the state: an irony for Hannibal, who like previous Barcid leaders had had little affinity for naval war. Neither he nor, we may presume, any of his lieutenants was brought before the high court of 104 to answer for the débâcle. Even so this body, after forty years of compliance with the Barcids, was ready to assert itself as the leading force in the state.

Carthage after the peace: domination of the 'judges'

No doubt the court of 104, whose members were all senators, included many Barcid kinsmen and supporters (or ex-supporters), thanks to nearly two generations of Barcid ascendancy. Clearly, however, political dominance no longer lay with Hannibal's faction, even if he and it remained too influential to be attacked. Past supporters, maybe even some Barcid kinsmen, would find it prudent to form other attachments. In turn, the men elected as sufetes and other magistrates over the next few years would reflect the new alignments in the court and among the senate, The Mighty Ones. For example, new friends and allies could multiply around the aged Hanno the Great (if he still lived) and his friend Hasdrubal 'the Kid', the spokesman of the embassy sent to Rome after Zama. This Hasdrubal's sudden prominence suggests that Hannibal's opponents came to the fore at last. We hear nothing again of either man after 202, but it seems that before long a single non-Barcid group replaced Hannibal's family faction as the dominant force in the republic – not a welter of cliques competing antagonistically for offices. For by 196 'the judges', as Livy calls them, were a united enough political caste to prompt bitterly cogent criticism, including by Hannibal.

The catastrophe of defeat sidelined Hannibal, though he may have continued as general (for a time) if a fourth-century AD writer from Roman Africa correctly reports that 'he replanted much of Africa with olive-trees, using his troops, whose idleness he considered problematic for the republic and its leaders.'[32] The countryside from Carthage to Sicca, and maybe elsewhere, did need attention after Scipio's extensive plunderings. Nepos claims that Hannibal now campaigned in Africa, but this cannot be true – there were no foes to fight and he would have needed Roman permission, of which we hear nothing. More likely with his remaining troops he spent much of 201 reimposing Carthage's control over her Libyan subjects inland at least as far as Sicca, and eastwards as far as the Gulf of Sirte. It would be natural, too, to make a start at repairing the damage done by Scipio's and Masinissa's campaigns, including replanting olive trees. These labours, moreover, if done with common sense would benefit all Carthaginian landowners, not just Barcid relatives and friends. This was wise if he wanted to ease political resentments.

At Carthage, though, he was not always tactful. Besides his rough handling of Gisco the diehard, another story of acerbic behaviour is told of the moment when the first treaty-payment (compensation for plundering the Roman supply ships) was being levied in 201. As Carthage's rich – many or most of them senators, no doubt – amid sighs and groans parted with some of their wealth, Hasdrubal the Kid saw Hannibal smiling at the scene. To Hasdrubal's angry criticism Hannibal replied (in Livy's account):

This smile you are criticising comes not from a joyful heart, but from one almost insane with suffering. The time for weeping was when our weapons were taken from us, our ships burned, and an interdiction placed on foreign wars – that was the blow that finished us off. But now, because tribute must be gathered from private sources, you are in mourning, as though you were attending the funeral of our state.[33]

A brief to restore the state's authority across Libya and encourage agriculture, keeping his remaining troops usefully busy until they could be paid off, may have been as welcome to him as to critics who found his presence at home difficult.

Nepos then has him step down from command in 200, which is plausible – even though Nepos imagines that Mago his brother was still alive and had to step down, too. Hannibal could not expect to continue indefinitely as general in peacetime, nor would it be politically astute. Meanwhile there was much to keep him busy in personal life, after thirty-five years' absence, though it is not known whether his Spanish wife Imilce, and the son that Silius Italicus says they had, were still alive. He was head of the Barcid family, which still included one or more of his sisters and quite likely nieces, nephews and even cousins. After thirty-five years, his own property affairs must have needed attention too. As mentioned earlier, we hear of an estate of his on the Emporia coast; he also owned a city house, and probably other properties urban and rural. He was a successful manager. By 195 he had great wealth, and enjoyed valuable contacts outside Africa, notably with Carthage's mother-city Tyre and other parts of the eastern Mediterranean. Leading Carthaginians quickly re-established ties of guest-friendship with eminent Romans too, and although none is known for any Barcid, the blank may be due merely to gaps (accidental or deliberate) in our information.

At Carthage Hannibal remained popular and well connected. Of his old friends, Mago the Samnite may still have been with him, for Nepos' report of a Mago sailing in later years to join him in exile, but dying en route, cannot be his brother (as Nepos thinks) but could be his friend. Silenus and Sosylus too, his Greek followers, may have stayed on at Carthage, since Nepos' comment that they stayed 'as long as fortune allowed' need not imply a parting of the ways right after Zama. As for the Barcid faction, it was shrunken in numbers, could no longer determine state policies, and probably failed to win many (or any) high offices after 202, but it continued to exist and to look to him as leader.

The 'judges', the new dominant group, whether led by Hasdrubal the Kid or someone else, did not endear themselves to their fellow citizens. Corruption and self-enrichment at public expense were of course scarcely novel at Carthage, but now they grew shamelessly rampant. A scandal tainted payment of the first instalment of the war-indemnity in 199 – the 200 talents of gold taken to Rome turned out to be seriously adulterated, forcing the envoys to borrow funds there to make up the balance. This particular fraud did not happen again; but other peculation reached plague proportions in just a few years. Exploitative and increasingly unpopular, the 'judges' stuck together like a mafia:

> the property, reputation and lives of everyone lay in their power. A man who crossed a member of that body found all of them against him, nor did someone fail to accuse him before a hostile judiciary.[34]

The faction made matters worse by putting the republic at odds with Masinissa. The cause of the dispute is not known, but it was used by the Romans in 195 as a pretext for an embassy to Carthage whose real aim was to attack Hannibal. Since he was not blamed for the dispute even when the envoys then denounced him, it appears that the problem arose before his sufeteship. Masinissa may well have been the party responsible, just as he was in later wrangles and no doubt for the same goal: a slice of territory or some other advantage at Carthage's expense. Still, for the anti-Barcid group, with its pro-Roman leanings, to be clashing with Carthage's powerful pro-Roman neighbour and be unable to solve the issue could only put it in a still more contemptible light.

By 197 the treasury was close to collapse. To pay the coming year's instalment of the war-indemnity, a special tax was mooted. In other words, citizens would have to pay out of their own pockets to make up for the thievery of the ruling group. The group's hold on office was not broken right away, but public discontent flowed to Hannibal's advantage. He stood for election as sufete, successfully, with an unknown colleague (probably a member of his group, since as sufete he gave Hannibal no trouble). In 196 he took office, and acted.

Hannibal, sufete of Carthage

Unexpectedly, the republic's shoddy finances were not the first bone of contention. When Hannibal moved to investigate them, he was defied by a magistrate whom Livy calls a 'quaestor'. Roman quaestors were junior financial magistrates, so this was presumably an equivalent office-holder at Carthage – an elected one, since the man was relying not only on support from the dominant faction but on his own right to enter the judges' ranks (the court of 104) when his term expired. This abruptly shifted the focus of dispute in a direction which, it seems, Hannibal's opponents had not foreseen. His political flair was as adroit as his old battlefield tactics. He hauled the recalcitrant before the citizen assembly and used the incident as a lever to propose – and then carry – a law that removed judges' lifetime tenure, made membership annually electable, and banned re-election for a second consecutive year.

A sufete had the right to put a matter to the people if he and The Mighty Ones disagreed over it. Livy's compressed narrative says nothing about the Carthaginian senate, but its majority's hostility to reform must be assumed if the faction based on the 'judges' was indeed dominant – even though we may reasonably expect that some senators, and even some judges, were still in Hannibal's faction. With all the judges now up for election, the excitement of reform very likely brought political advantage to the Barcid group. How the first judicial elections went is not recorded but, as soon as the law itself was carried, all opposition to the sufete collapsed. He returned to the question of the finances, carried out thorough investigations, and then enacted reforms that both cleaned up the treasury and recovered much of the money stolen. The mooted special tax was dropped. Nepos writes that Hannibal himself imposed fresh taxes, but this looks like a misunderstanding; any new impositions would have destroyed the sufete's credit. Livy, more plausibly, indicates that by stopping embezzlement and negligence he kept his promise to enrich the republic.

Just possibly, Hannibal's activity in office extended even to Carthage's physical development. A new residential and commercial district was built, around this time, on previously unused ground on the southern slope of the Byrsa hill. It boasted broad, carefully laid out and well-drained streets, lined by handsome buildings for apartments and shops, with Greek-style interior conveniences such as peristyle courtyards. Hannibal was certainly familiar with city planning, after such successful Barcid projects as Acra Leuce and New Carthage. Until his financial reforms took hold, though, state finances were too straitened to allow public building on any large scale. Nor was it all that desirable when men of means could pay their own building costs – as many were certainly able to do by 196. His rôle, if he did play one, would be to initiate or at least encourage the work, supervise planning and maybe even designs, and (always important) keep the red tape to a minimum. The district (nicknamed the 'quartier Hannibal' by its archaeologists) would prosper until the catastrophe of 146.[35]

All these measures required time and matching energy. How Hannibal enforced his reforms is not recorded, but to do it successfully he had to have reliable and energetic support – at every level, not simply from intermittent meetings of voters in the assembly. He plainly had it. The Barcid faction regained its influence, thanks now to civic reform rather than military prowess, and its opponents were paralysed. The elections for the new judiciary almost certainly confirmed this, even though Hannibal himself did not seek re-election as sufete (he may of course have been elected one of the new judges). For to attack him, the opposing faction had to look outside Carthage altogether.

Indirect evidence suggests that his reforms succeeded. Five years later the republic felt able to offer a financial windfall to the Romans, who by then were at war with Antiochus III, the ruler of the eastern world from the Aegean to the Indus: Carthage would repay the balance of her war-indemnity – forty years' instalments – at once, while also supporting the Roman war effort with large gifts of grain. In other words, whereas in 197 a special tax had been mooted to raise just 200 talents, in 191 the republic was able to offer 8,000 talents in a lump sum (a four thousand per cent improvement). Commerce and agriculture were of course reviving, which helped to increase public resources, but it must be equally true that far less revenue was now being creamed off en route to the treasury. This fits both Livy's and Nepos' reports about the effect of Hannibal's tax reforms. Other improving measures may have been brought in after 195, but it was Hannibal who started the process and, quite likely, enacted the major part of it.

In politics, the Barcid group remained influential even after Hannibal himself was forced into exile, but more striking is that, even without the Barcids in later decades, Carthage continued to enjoy a vigorously varied political life that lasted (if sometimes with more vigour than judgement) until the last clash with Rome.

In other words, the faction of 'judges' did not recover oligarchic supremacy after 195. It or its successor had to compete for office and influence with others. Whether Hannibal's own electoral reform endured or was amended, his sufeteship opened a new, more open style of politics which was to endure.

In one extraordinary year, Hannibal did more for the political and economic health of his city than in twenty years of generalship in the field. Why he chose not to seek re-election is unknown: at its simplest, perhaps to set an example by obeying the same principle that he had applied to the judges. As noticed just now, the new arrangements meant that his enemies could not automatically recover supremacy; and so he had no need to fear biased prosecution once he left office. What he could not control, as sufete or ex-sufete, was hostile intrigue. No doubt he knew that as soon as he launched his reforms – or even before them – his opponents would let their friends at Rome know, and that this would involve exaggerations and lies. All he could do was to take precautions in case a crisis erupted, and maybe to hope that more principled Roman leaders – such as Scipio Africanus – would prevent him being victimised.

The flight of Hannibal

Scipio did strongly oppose victimising him:

> He considered it quite unbecoming to the honour of the Roman people to underwrite the hatred of Hannibal's accusers and involve state prestige in Carthage's factional politics; to regard defeating Hannibal in war as inadequate unless, like prosecutors, they now swore lies against him and put him on trial.[36]

But opinion had turned in the Roman senate. Tensions were beginning to rise with Antiochus III, so Hannibal's foes astutely alleged that he was secretly negotiating with the Great King to take

Carthage into his camp for a war of revenge. Even though Scipio was honorary first senator, the best he could finally do was have a senatorial friend, Terentius Culleo – once a prisoner-of-war at Carthage – chosen as one (the most junior) of three envoys sent over to Carthage in 195. One of the others was the son of Hannibal's old foe Marcellus.

Arriving out of the blue, but already primed by the anti-Barcids, the envoys claimed to have come to settle the dispute with Masinissa. Livy writes that

> this was generally believed. Hannibal alone realised that he was the Romans' target, and that peace had been granted to the Carthaginians on the stipulation of unforgiving war against him alone.[37]

The city's authorities showed no enthusiasm for this unexpected visitation, but Hannibal knew that, if the envoys demanded his handover or trial, they could not be resisted. His preparations were ready. That same night, with two companions – maybe Silenus and Sosylus, or other friends – he rode away from Carthage for the last time. By the next day he had reached his coastal estate in Emporia, where a ship was waiting for him at anchor, and he stood to sea. The military precision of his departure shows that he had long foreseen just such a need. Even so, the immediate readiness of all the necessary elements for flight – horses waiting outside the city gates, portable wealth packed and ready, and the ship riding in his roadstead fully equipped and crewed – hints at advance notice. We might wonder whether Scipio or some other sympathetic Roman (Cincius Alimentus?) had sent a warning ahead by fast messenger.

At the offshore island of Cercina (Kerkennah), he reportedly prevented word of his whereabouts being relayed to the mainland by visiting merchants, by laying on a marvellously bibulous party for everyone in the port – magistrates and merchants included – and then setting sail by night while the revellers slept off their drink. At Carthage the authorities, unenthusiastic but unable to refuse, gave in to the envoys' pressure and declared him an exile, seizing his property and demolishing his house, but no reprisals were taken against his relatives or friends. In due course, Hannibal reached Tyre, where he was received as an honoured guest. It was only a stopover, all the same. His goal was the court of Antiochus III, the ruler who was plainly to be the next great enemy of the Romans.

CHAPTER 8

HANNIBAL IN EXILE
(195–183)

H annibal was fifty-two when he left his homeland for the second and final time, a man still in his prime. The dozen years that remained were adventurous, varied and full of long-remembered stories. Yet equally they were a disappointing coda for the man who had conquered half of Spain, won over half of Italy, brought terror upon the Romans, established his name as Alexander the Great's equal, and constructively reformed his country. Once the elected general and leader of a republic, he had to attend a succession of spoilt monarchs who treated him as a useful but disposable client – a situation made for a Roman satirist to lampoon:

> Ah, glory. Of course he's beaten
> And hurries headlong into exile, and there
> Our mighty and marvellous client sits by the palace,
> Till it shall please Bithynia's despot to wake.[38]

The court and council of the Great King

Even if he had had some contacts with King Antiochus, they were not up-to-date or intimate, for only when he arrived at Antioch in Syria did he find that the king had moved to Ephesus on the Aegean. There is no sign, either, that Antiochus had really thought of attracting Carthage as an ally – or now treated the exile as an indispensable lieutenant for a coming war. When Hannibal reached Ephesus, the king was still trying to negotiate his differences with Rome. It was some time before his new guest was invited to the royal council and, when he was, his urgings for a pre-emptive war did not appeal.

He proposed that he should sail with 100 royal warships, 10,000 foot and 1,000 horse, first to Africa to win over Carthage, then on to northern Italy to raise war there against the Romans. Meanwhile Antiochus should move his main forces into Greece, ally with the Aetolian League (once allied to the Romans, but now hostile) and prepare to cross to Italy. Hannibal's basic principles were perceptive: the Romans could, indeed, be beaten only in Italy and only by a massive coalition. Too much else in the plan, though, was faulty – not just its relegation of the king and his envious generals to second place. Hannibal's own experience had taught that against Rome a far larger invasion force than 11,000 was essential. Nor were Gauls and Ligurians effective auxiliaries by themselves; yet the chance of any of the Italian allies defecting yet again from Rome was slight. Antiochus, in turn, had nothing like 100 ships available for a risky expedition and showed no interest in acquiring more.

Hannibal, meanwhile, rather unfortunately weakened his impact at court in various ways. Cicero tells a story of courtiers at Ephesus taking their celebrity friend to an extended lecture on generalship by Phormio, a noted philosopher, only to receive a tart Hannibalic comment afterwards: he had seen plenty of old drivellers often, but never any who in drivelling outdid Phormio. Much worse for him were his friendly conversations at Ephesus in 193 with Villius Tappulus, a former consul and head of a Roman embassy to Antiochus. Villius was perhaps an agreeable dinner partner, but in fact each man was using the opportunity to sound the other on prospects for peace and war in Italy, Africa and the eastern empire. The camaraderie, all the same, did not go down well in the royal

Imaginative nineteenth-century woodcut of the general and army at the top of the pass, gazing at the plains of Italy.

circle; it was what caused Hannibal to tell the king the famous story of his boyhood oath, in order to prove his lasting antipathy to the Romans.

Even if Antiochus was appeased (as we are told he was), he allowed the exile no more influence than before. In 193, moreover, a last effort to restore Hannibal's fortunes at home failed when Aristo, a merchant and confidant of his from Tyre, made a clumsy attempt to take help to the Barcid faction but was soon expelled from Carthage. Hannibal's flight had deprived his supporters both of their leader and, clearly, of their briefly restored ascendancy. The episode did nothing for his credit with his hosts; his own offer to return to Carthage for the same purpose was not accepted.

Another Hannibal story was told of these years at Ephesus. Supposedly he met Scipio Africanus once again, this time on an embassy to the Great King. Naturally they discussed military matters, rather as Hannibal had done with Cincius; and Scipio fished for a compliment by asking whom Hannibal judged the greatest general of all.

> 'Alexander the Great [replied Hannibal], for he routed uncountable armies with small forces and reached the furthest shores [of the world].' When Scipio then asked whom he would rank second, he said 'Pyrrhus.' ... To Scipio's query as to the third, he said, 'Myself, without a doubt.' Then Scipio broke into laughter and added, 'What would you say had you beaten me?' – 'Then,' replied Hannibal, 'I would say I was superior to Alexander, and Pyrrhus, and all other generals.'[39]

In reality, Scipio was never on such an embassy, and so the tale is usually judged some later writer's fancy. We need not go that far. Villius is quite likely to have questioned his awesome but genial fellow guest on such a topic, including how he judged Scipio. If the answers were at all worth reporting when the embassy went home, it would not be hard (or take long) for tradition to replace the forgettable Villius with Scipio himself as Hannibal's questioner.

When war with the Romans did finally come during 192, king and court sailed to winter at the coastal fortress town of Demetrias in Thessaly, where Hannibal urged a revised invasion plan. His own rôle was minimised: the king should win Philip V of Macedon as an ally or keep him neutral, use the royal fleet to command the Ionian and Tyrrhenian seas, concentrate the royal army in Epirus, and then invade Italy. This made much more strategic sense, apart from the hope of recruiting Philip (recently humbled in his own second war with Rome, and uninterested in becoming a Roman target to the benefit of a rival king). Polite applause in council, though, was all Hannibal received – that and a paradoxical, almost insulting commission as, of all things, a naval commodore in the east, sharing in operations against Rome's naval ally Rhodes.

Antiochus' obvious lack of interest in what could have been his trump card against the Romans remains surprising. Livy claims that, when invited to the royal council, Hannibal was asked his opinion last, an obvious slight. Livy puts the king's attitude down to fear, fostered by the royal generals, that Hannibal might conspire to take his throne. In reality, it is almost impossible that the king believed, even for a moment, that an outsider could achieve this against a well-established royal family and Greek governing élite. True, his generals were far from enthusiastic about the newcomer, so perhaps the military establishment of the eastern empire – all Greek professionals – simply resented any serious rôle being given to a 'barbarian' loser. The king could all the same have overborne them, but he himself was fairly obviously unimpressed by anything the great exile had to offer, and chose a different strategy, meeting the enemy in Greece with the Aetolians as allies. That strategy proved catastrophic: Antiochus was soon driven out of Greece, Aetolian resistance collapsed, Philip gave the Romans supplies and safe passage through his kingdom, and by late 190 a Roman army, with Scipio himself as lieutenant to his brother the consul in command, had crossed to Asia Minor.

Hannibal meanwhile was at sea, in more senses than one. He had no problem with raising a fleet from the Phoenician cities such as Tyre, but when he sailed westwards with it during summer 190 he was confronted off Side, on the Pamphylian coast, by a smaller fleet under Eudamus of Rhodes. Hannibal had an unblooded force and no naval experience. Eudamus defeated the makeshift commodore with serious losses and shut him up in a nearby port. Before the following winter ended, the large but ill-assorted army of Antiochus III was shattered by the Romans and their ally Eumenes, king of

Pergamum, at Magnesia (inland from Smyrna), and the king sued for terms. The terms, imposed by Scipio, cost Antiochus all his territories in Asia Minor and exacted a war-indemnity fifty per cent larger than Carthage was paying. Another stipulation was that Hannibal must be handed over to the victors.

Wandering years: Armenia and Bithynia

The Romans had not forgotten how Hannibal had eluded them six years earlier, and he had compounded the offence by taking service with their latest opponent. Antiochus, a reigning monarch, was punished and then forgiven, but the exile was not. Had he been taken to Rome, death in the Tullianum prison beneath the Capitol would most likely have been his fate, like other captured enemies (including, one day, Masinissa's great-grandson Jugurtha). Scipio's own attitude towards him may have changed; or had it? Until the peace was ratified, an armistice applied; and it turned out to last a full year, till early 188. Neither the Romans nor Antiochus interfered meanwhile with the Mediterranean world's most distinguished exile, who made his own arrangements for leaving the Great King's court.

According to his biographer Nepos, he sailed to Crete and then to Bithynia, but Nepos ignores a notable intervening episode which both Strabo and Plutarch record. First he travelled still further east to Armenia, in the mountains and valleys of today's north-eastern Turkey and north-western Iran. If Silenus and Sosylus had been with him still, now would be the likeliest time when he parted company with them, for their devotion – or simply their age – might well not extend to so uncomfortable and risky a venture. Armenia had just broken free of the defeated eastern empire to become two independent states, the northern one ruled by its old governor Artaxias. Hannibal may have felt relatively secure with a patron owing no favours to Antiochus (who died in 187) or his successors. Artaxias had no military tasks for him, perhaps purposely; a new ruler giving military power to a rootless military genius might well seem to be running an unnecessary risk. Instead, Hannibal pursued a different Barcid tradition, surveying a site for a new capital on the banks of the river Araxes:

> observing the great natural capacities and the pleasantness of the site, then lying unoccupied and neglected, he drew a model of a city for it, and bringing Artaxias thither, showed it to him and encouraged him to build. At which the king, being pleased and desiring him to oversee the work, erected a large and stately city which was called after his own name [Artaxata, on the banks of the river Araxes beneath Mt Ararat], and made metropolis of Armenia.[40]

Hannibal's city, Artashat today, still stands 20 miles south of Yerevan.

All the same, any Carthaginian would find limited appeal in freezing winters and idleness in a landlocked mountain kingdom, dominated by feuding baronial lords (as it would be for a millennium and more). Artaxias in turn, interested in being recognised by Rome, may have cooled towards his controversial guest. By 186 Hannibal was on the move, passing quietly through Syria to Phoenicia (so it seems), to obtain a ship and crew for travel westward.

Probably now he stopped for some time at Gortyn in Crete, as Nepos tells it, 'there to decide where he should betake himself', and where, as Nepos tells it, he showed yet again his resourcefulness under pressure. Aware that the proverbially covetous Cretans were eyeing his portable gold and silver, he ostentatiously dedicated jars brimming with precious metals in the local temple, while a humdrum pair of bronze statues stood in his courtyard. 'The Gortynians kept a careful guard over the temple, not so much against others as against Hannibal himself, lest he carry the jars away.' Once he had sailed away, of course – taking the statues, hollow and packed with his wealth – they found nothing in the jars but lead under the top layer of valuables.[41]

By now the Mediterranean was closing against Hannibal. The only ruler still willing to give him sanctuary was Prusias, king of the small but rich state of Bithynia in north-west Asia Minor. Hannibal acquired a villa at a seaside hamlet called Libyssa, on the road to the Bosphorus 22 Roman miles (about 18 miles today) from the royal capital of Nicomedia, modern Izmit. Always alive to the risk of treachery, including from his Bithynian host, he fitted out the villa with seven secret exits. Yet he did not shun Prusias' court or ignore the wider world, in which the Romans' influence now stretched – when they chose to exert it – from the Atlantic to the river Euphrates. A later author, the encyclopaedist Pliny the Elder, credits him with designing a new city for the king, perhaps his first commission on arriving; Prusias must have heard about Artaxata. It was suitably named Prusa (Bursa today, near the Sea of Marmara) and, reminiscent of Artaxata, at the foot of a mountain, Bithynia's own Mt Olympus.[42]

Hannibal, writer and Bithynian commodore

He also kept up contacts outside Bithynia and composed some works in Greek, probably on military matters. The Rhodians were sent an account of a recent and destructive Roman war against Antiochus III's allies the Galatians, who dwelt in Asia Minor's interior. Some Galatians were friends and allies of Prusias, too, which may explain the choice of topic and his sources of information, though not why the Rhodians were his addressees. It may simply be that a Rhodian family or families enjoyed a bond of guest-friendship with the Barcids. The Rhodians, moreover, had benefited substantially from the settlement of 188 with Antiochus. Hannibal may have intended a warning about their new patrons.

In recent years, Roman power had rolled like a tidal wave across the eastern Mediterranean, and the stunned states and realms of those lands were bewildered, angry, and unsure how to come to terms with it. A letter from 'Hannibal, king of the Carthaginians', to the Athenians – clearly invented – in which the hero reminds them of Cannae and promises the downfall of Roman rule over the Greeks, survives in a papyrus fragment tentatively dated to the 180s. Not long afterwards, a contemporary historian, Antisthenes (interestingly, a Rhodian), put apocalyptic, not to mention apoplectic, prophecies of Rome's destruction by invading nations of the east into the mouths of both a Greek general and of Scipio himself, supposedly on his arrival in Greece in 190; they are preserved in extracts made three hundred years later. Hannibal's own work was surely critical of the Roman general Manlius Vulso's misbehaviour and greed (Manlius was severely criticised at Rome itself for his actions) and possibly critical overall of Roman actions in the east. We may wonder whether he included the famous, and true, story of the Galatian princess Chiomara, captured and raped by a centurion, who as soon as she was ransomed had her retainers kill the Roman on the spot, then took his head to her husband to prove her honour.

Prusias did have a war for Hannibal to take part in, against his neighbour and enemy (and close ally of Rome) Eumenes, king of Pergamum. Again, the exile had to try his hand at sea, in 186 or 185, leading Prusias' outnumbered fleet against the Pergamene king's in the Sea of Marmara. Of this more Hannibal stories are told. Aiming to kill or capture Eumenes in the battle, he ascertained which ship the king was in by sending over a personal message (which proved scurrilous) to the enemy fleet under flag of truce; then, narrowly failing to take ship and king together, he drove him ashore out of the battle. Next, his men hurled clay pots stuffed with poisonous snakes onto the other enemy decks, gaining victory through the resulting panic. The opening unsuccessful ruse may be true, as the victory certainly was, but the snakes' rôle looks like an exaggeration or invention (if they were so venomous, Hannibal's own men would have found it dangerous to capture Pergamene ships). Nepos' further claim of him going on to win several battles on land seems unlikely too, unless mere skirmishes are meant. By contrast Prusias, leading his army, was defeated by Eumenes, despite having the warlike Galatians as allies and receiving some covert help from Philip V. But the war dragged on.

Death in exile

Finally the Romans intervened. An embassy arrived in Asia, late in 183 or early in 182, led by the formidable Titus Quinctius Flamininus, who had crushed Philip a decade and a half earlier and imposed peace on Macedon and the Greeks. Peace was now imposed on the warring kings, to Eumenes' benefit. In addition, Flamininus called on Prusias to hand over Hannibal.

Some accounts of this event depict Flamininus as learning, to his surprise, of Hannibal's presence in Bithynia only when he arrived. Yet, after building a new royal city, commanding a fleet, and publishing a historical pamphlet for the Rhodians, Hannibal's whereabouts must have been quite well known (as another writer, Plutarch, realises). Nepos, by contrast, has Eumenes' brother at Rome announce his whereabouts to the senate, prompting a decree that authorised Flamininus to act. The decree looks likely, even if the senate did not need to be told where to find Hannibal. If Flamininus did feel surprise at Nicomedia, it may have been to learn that his quarry lived not in elusively distant seclusion, but close by.

Prusias may have been embarrassed at having to betray a guest-

friend, but he could not risk offending the Romans. He allowed
Hannibal no warning but surrounded the villa with troops, placing
detachments at every one of its secret exits. Then officers entered
the courtyard, calling for Hannibal. Trapped, ageing and defiant, the
Carthaginian, in Livy's sympathetic telling,

> called for the poison which he had prepared well in advance ...
> 'Let us free the people of Rome from their lingering anxiety,'
> he said, 'since they find it too long a process to wait for an old
> man's death. ... These men's ancestors forewarned Pyrrhus, an
> enemy under arms with an army in Italy, to be on his guard
> against poison; but these have sent an ex-consul as an envoy to
> incite Prusias to the heinous act of murdering a guest.' Then,
> calling down curses on Prusias' head and his kingdom, and
> calling upon the gods of hospitality to witness the king's breach
> of faith, he drained the cup.[43]

Juvenal the satirist has him carry the poison in a signet-ring
(though it would still need to be mixed in a cup of wine):

> An end to that soul which once had upheaved the world
> Will come not from swords, not stones or arms: vengeance
> For Cannae, the nemesis of so much blood –
> A ring.[44]

Livy gives Hannibal a rhetorical speech of drama and pathos; we
should not doubt that he spoke seriously (with his household to
witness), perhaps bitterly, as he readied himself for suicide. His
appeal to the gods rings true, and it was a suitable end. Hannibal
entered history taking an oath before the gods because of the
Romans: and, again because of them, left it calling for one last time
on heaven. He was sixty-four.

Flamininus did not remove or dishonour the body. A tumulus was
built at Libyssa as the exile's resting-place and remained famous over

centuries to come. Nearly four hundred years later another North African, the emperor Septimius Severus, would adorn it splendidly with white marble, though today no trace of the monument remains. At Rome, reaction was muted or indifferent; partly because, in a striking irony, the greatest Roman of his time – Scipio Africanus, the victor of Zama – was mortally ill or had just died. In time, the Romans' hatred would change to reluctant admiration blended with lingering hostility: and, by another irony, Hannibal's fame would be stamped on the memory of Roman civilisation and its heirs by the work, above all, of a Roman historian.

CHAPTER 9

HANNIBAL: MEMORY AND MYTH

Cicero mentions a Roman proverb denoting the ultimate emergency: 'Hannibal ad portas!'[45] 'Hannibal at the gates' of Rome stamped himself forever into Roman memory. Even Pyrrhus, the other great Hellenistic invader, had not come as close. No other foreign enemy remained longer on Italian soil or posed a more imminent threat to Rome's survival – or caused more Roman deaths. In turn, the more irresistibly powerful the Romans became, the more they admired as well as resented the man who had almost prevented this from happening.

Could Hannibal have won? The modern consensus is that he could not. The Romans, it is argued, were too many, too stubborn and too resourceful; his own people few, unwarlike or – on another interpretation – unenthusiastic. All the same, this view is not very plausible on the evidence we have.

Carthaginians themselves may have been fewer in numbers than Roman citizens (though even this is not certain), but together with their allies and subjects were roughly equal to the Romans and theirs: about three and a half to four million souls on either side. Militarily they were not outnumbered until late in the war. In 215–214, as noted earlier, they had some 150,000 troops in arms and the Romans about the same. In 207, with about 65,000 Roman citizens and as many allies under arms (on the evidence of our chief sources, Polybius and Livy), Hannibal's side (judging from the same sources) still fielded 150,000. At sea, where the Carthaginians started the war with a massive inferiority of fewer than a hundred seaworthy warships to 220 Roman, they rebuilt the navy; there were as many as 130 ships in Syracusan waters in 212. Financing the war, in turn, may have brought increasing strains just as it did at Rome, but as late as 205 funds were still available to lavish on Mago's Ligurian expedition.

For unenthusiastic home backing there is virtually no evidence – only the self-interested claims in 203 by the prostrate Carthaginians and the unhappily returning Hannibal, taken up later on by historians clearly for their own argumentative purposes. The Carthaginians, under Hannibal's direction according to Polybius, took opportunity after opportunity to intensify the struggle or recover from setbacks – drawing in the north Italian Gauls, Philip V, Syphax and even Syphax's heir; battling the Scipios, elder and younger, for thirteen years in Spain; seeking to recover Sardinia; supporting Syracuse and other anti-Roman Sicilian cities. At the very end, after Zama, there were still Carthaginians refusing to admit defeat.

Polybius has his own explanations for why Hannibal did not win. First, because the Romans' political and military systems, and civic qualities, were superior – their constitution had not become democratic and thereby weaker, they did not rely on mercenary troops, and they were fighting for their homeland and families. Yet if democratic usages were truly a demerit, his own emphasis on Hannibal's powerful control of Punic affairs should prove that such a situation did not exist at Carthage. Similarly, his own emphatic praise for the quality of Hannibal's army (which was largely mercenary) as well as for his leadership undermines his assumption that such forces were inherently inferior. The superiority or inferiority of civic qualities, in turn, is a subjective judgement, and all that we can say is that the Carthaginians showed no lack of spirit or seriousness in fighting the war.

Elsewhere Polybius makes a different claim:

there can be no fear in saying that, if he had reserved his attack upon the Romans until he had first subdued other parts of the world, there is not one of his projects which would have eluded his grasp. As it was, he began with those whom he should have attacked last, and accordingly began and ended his career with them.[46]

In other words, for Polybius Hannibal struck too soon. Yet this is not much better than a platitude. Had Hannibal really managed to conquer much of the world outside Italy, the Romans would indeed have been overwhelmed; but Polybius cannot seriously mean that before confronting them he should – or could – have conquered Gaul, Macedon and Greece, for instance, along with the rest of Spain. Even to follow up the conquest of northern Spain – which he did largely achieve – by anticipating Julius Caesar in Gaul would have been very risky, not to mention time-consuming, and would pretty certainly have aroused Roman intervention anyway. More likely Polybius is just rephrasing, in more sweeping terms, a much earlier comment: that in Spain Hannibal had meant to avoid a clash with Rome until he had conquered all the rest of the country, 'according to Hamilcar's plans and advice' – alluding to the alleged and improbable Barcid scheme for a revenge-war. If so, his claim remains not very profound.

Victory and defeat, like other human endeavours when two sides are well matched, are not usually decided by one or even a couple of factors. Carthage's lack of serious naval forces at the start was certainly a factor. The earlier Barcid leaders had let naval strength lapse; this not only took years to rectify materially, but meant that the continuity of her naval war-skills had been broken. The best Hannibal could do was to have the home authorities build new warships – and for them the artificial ports, perhaps – but he himself showed limited appreciation of naval potential, and the officers who actually commanded the Punic fleets were none of them impressive.

This was equally and damagingly true of most of Carthage's field commanders. True, Hannibal's brothers were energetic and Hasdrubal, at least, was a good organiser, but they and many others – notably Hasdrubal son of Gisco, the Barcids' nephew Hanno, and Himilco the general in Sicily confronting Marcellus – did not match vigour with many victories. Even though, under Hannibal's direct command, officers such as his brother Mago or nephew Hanno performed outstandingly, on their own they and others missed opportunities – for example, failing to exploit fully the destruction of the elder Scipios in Spain – and lost battles. Dispiritingly, a non-Carthaginian officer with promising all-round abilities, Mottones, aroused so much resentment from Himilco in Sicily that, as mentioned above, he finally defected to the Romans. Hannibal was not responsible for his colleagues' limitations, but (with rare exceptions such as Mottones) he seems not to have sought out and promoted fresh talent alongside or in place of them. Political needs may have played a part in this immobility: very probably, for instance, with Hasdrubal son of Gisco. In any case the results were not beneficial.

Hannibal himself never lost a battle before Zama, but he too missed opportunities and made miscalculations. As his was the principal theatre of operations, these flaws contributed substantially to why he did not win the war. The most momentous are notoriously the hardest to explain: the sixty per cent loss of troops in the march from the Pyrenees to north Italy, his failure to coordinate operations in any way with his brother when Hasdrubal came into Italy in 207, and – most debated of all – why he did not march on Rome after Cannae, or indeed after Trasimene. Had matters been managed differently in any of these situations, his prospects for final victory would have been immensely stronger.

They might also have improved had he received some of the forces sent to other theatres – Spain, Sardinia, Sicily and Liguria – between 215 and 205, a total of well over 70,000 men. Apart from Spain, none of these theatres ought to have been regarded as more vital to the war than his own. As Carthage's chief general, responsibility for these military decisions was his. Even if he thought that Italian recruitment could maintain his own forces, it ought to have been obvious by 211 at latest that this was not enough to overcome the Romans; Carthaginian forces, however, continued to be sent elsewhere. Hasdrubal's invasion in 207 and Mago's in 205 were, in effect, attempts to launch a second front to divide and disrupt the enemy, but they remained so distant from their brother that they merely divided and weakened the Carthaginian effort.

Some of these questionable measures were reactions to the Romans' indomitable resistance, symbolised in the traditional depictions of Fabius the Delayer and the experienced and level-headed Roman senate. Such idealisation is overdrawn – it was the senate that wanted Cannae, for instance, and Fabius who resolutely opposed Scipio invading Africa – but solid leadership did restore the fortunes of Rome. The disastrous losses of 218 to 216 were made good; strategy and tactics were recast; invading Spain distracted the Carthaginians (it would have been still better in 218 to let Spain alone and invade Africa). Scipio apart, no Roman general was equal to Hannibal – but many were a match for other Punic commanders.

Against Hannibal, trial and error and catastrophe taught the lesson of avoiding pitched battle as far as possible and instead putting pressure on his allies, such as Capua, and his lieutenants, like Hanno. This reached the point where Capua could be tightly besieged and Hannibal's own relief attempts swatted aside, like an irrelevant though tiresome gadfly. As a result, even a Roman disaster like the second battle of Herdonea in 210, equivalent in slaughter to Trasimene, had little impact on the strategic situation.

Marcellus took matters further, dogging and harassing Hannibal's army to curtail his freedom of action, and accepting battles which the Roman general probably had no expectation of winning, but which inflicted further attrition – physical and psychological. The Romans then produced Scipio Africanus: 'the fate-chosen leader of this war' as Livy terms him.[47] It was not inevitable that Scipio would defeat Hannibal in battle, but he was the first Roman commander to match him in ability. Scipio's achievements in Spain and then in Africa, between 209 and 203, ended any hope of a Carthaginian victory in the war. Hannibal fought Zama to win a compromise peace.

A long-held view has been that Carthage's defeat was historically desirable. Supposedly, Punic civilisation was limited, uncreative, fixated on money-making, and shackled by a sombrely pessimistic religion. By contrast the Romans were emerging into the light of Greek culture, which they would hand on to future ages. Such a verdict ignored facts. In real life, Carthaginians were increasingly Hellenised by Hannibal's time: his own attainments, education and career were an example, not the exception. It is probable that Carthage's exposure to and borrowings from Greek civilisation were at least as great as contemporary Rome's. Hannibal and other Carthaginians moved easily among Greeks and Greek-speakers; and Carthaginians enjoyed guest-friendships with leading Romans – possibly too with leading Greeks. Fifty-five years after Hannibal's death, a Carthaginian philosopher called Hasdrubal would become one of the most distinguished heads of the Academy at Athens, under the Greek name Clitomachus. Punic gods were equated with Greek ones, as the treaty with Philip V, in particular, shows. Even war-elephants, Hannibal's trademark in popular memory, were a Hellenistic borrowing.

Greeks and Romans did complain about Punic perfidy and superstitions when it suited propaganda or self-congratulation

– just as, for example, Athenians complained of Spartans' failings for the same purposes, and Romans about the slimy morals of Greeks generally. Contrastingly, in Hannibal's own lifetime a Roman comedy, Plautus' *Poenulus*, could portray an elderly merchant of Carthage (named Hanno, of course) as both a funny foreign-speaker and a sympathetic father seeking his lost daughters, while both the hero and heroine are Carthaginians. No ancient writer depicts, hints, or indeed imagines the Punic wars in racial or fundamentalist terms. Like Hannibal himself, everyone at the time and after judged them – rightly – to be contests *de dignitate atque imperio*, 'for honour and power'.

Not only is it unwarranted to see a Carthaginian victory bringing down a dark night of barbarism on the western Mediterranean: very probably it would not even have imposed some type of Near Eastern culture. Carthage's growing involvement with Hellenism would have been accelerated if Hannibal had achieved domination over Rome and Italy, themselves increasingly Hellenised. She would inevitably, too, have been drawn into close and active relations with the Hellenistic states, as Rome was to be after 201. Hannibal, at the head of the combined strength of Punic Africa, Italy and Spain, would not have had greater difficulty in bringing the eastern Mediterranean under Punic hegemony than the Romans – without Carthage – were to have. The poet Horace's famous dictum about the cultural impact on Rome would have come true for Hannibal's city instead: 'conquered Greece captured her wild conqueror'. Hannibal's failed grand expedition is thus one of history's most intriguing might-have-beens.

Where he did succeed was as military leader and inspired winner of battles. This aspect – including the elephants and the epic crossing of the Alps – is the one which most observers have found and always will find the most fascinating. That is something of a paradox, since elephants figured in only his earliest victories, the Tagus and the

Trebia, and then, damagingly, at Zama; while the Alpine losses were a near-disaster for his invasion. Of course, fascination with the great victories of 218 to 216 – combining as they did sagacious choice of ground, inspired arrangement of units, and shattering surprises – is understandable. The manoeuvres at Cannae, above all, have stimulated field commanders and theorists alike even in modern times, inspiring most famously Count von Schlieffen's pre-1914 war-plan against France. Few imitations (least of all Schlieffen's) have succeeded nearly as well.

All the same, concentrating on the great victories undervalues other aspects of Hannibal's career. Polybius' and Livy's insistence (even if exaggerated) on the unswerving loyalty of his variegated forces emphasises the quality of his leadership, which for fifteen years in the heartland of his enemies kept in being a military power that matched Rome's. More than that, he was the mastermind – as Polybius stresses – of the war effort and international diplomacy of Carthage:

> Of all that befell the Romans and Carthaginians, good or bad, the cause was one man and one mind – Hannibal. For it is notorious that he managed the Italian campaigns in person, and the Spanish by the agency of the elder of his brothers, Hasdrubal, and subsequently by that of Mago ... Again, he conducted the Sicilian campaign at first through Hippocrates and afterwards through Mottones the Libyan. So also in Greece and Illyria: [there] he was enabled to distract the attention of the Romans, thanks to his understanding with Philip.[48]

From the aftermath of Cannae in 216 to the defeat of Hasdrubal in 207, Hannibal made Carthage preponderant in the western Mediterranean, holding territories and maintaining alliances from the Atlantic to the Aegean. It was the apogee of Carthaginian power, and no one else could have brought it about.

His postwar achievements are usually played down when not just passed over. Even though we have only glimpses of events at Carthage after 201, the contrasting evidence of a floundering, oligarchically maladministered, and discontented state before his sufeteship, and a rapid rise to prosperity and relatively open political life afterwards, reinforces the reports in Livy and Nepos of important and successful reforms under his leadership. It might even be argued that his civilian sufeteship did more lasting good for Carthage than his twenty years of field command, whatever the unforgettable glories of Trasimene and Cannae.

Would Hannibal have had an even greater constructive impact on Carthage's history, and that of the Mediterranean, had he chosen from the start to avoid war with the Romans and devote his immense abilities to his country's peaceful wealth and strength? A Roman provocation might still have arisen, in time, but Carthage would have been even harder – or would have been impossible – to defeat. Hannibal in 220, however, was not the middle-aged ex-general of 196 who by then had seen both success and failure in plenty. Carthaginian experiences in the First Punic War, relations with the Romans afterwards, and awareness of his own youthful genius all but dictated how he would respond to Rome's challenge over Saguntum and the Ebro. That he came so near to succeeding in his grand enterprise, that eventual failure was due in considerable part (though not solely) to his own miscalculations, and that despite final defeat his memory remains vivid today as one of the world's leading commanders, are the most memorable measures of the quality of Hannibal.

BIBLIOGRAPHY

1. Translations used in the text

Appian, tr. H. White (Loeb Classical Library, vol. 4: 1912)

Dio, tr. E. Cary (Loeb Classical Library, vol. 2: 1914)

Diodorus, tr. R.M. Geer and F.R. Walton (Loeb Classical Library, vols 10 and 11: 1954, 1957)

Livy, tr. J.C. Yardley, *Livy: Hannibal's War: Books 21–30*, with introduction and notes by D. Hoyos (Oxford, 2006); and *Livy: The Dawn of the Roman Empire: Books 31–40*, with introduction and notes by W. Heckel (Oxford, 1997); by permission of the translator

Plutarch, tr. John Dryden and others (London, 1683–86)

Polybius, tr. E.S. Shuckburgh (2 vols: London, 1889)

Cicero, Juvenal, Nepos, Silius Italicus and Victor, tr. by the author

2. Selected modern studies in English

The range of books in English on Hannibal and his times is very wide. Some of the most reliable and stimulating are the following:

The Cambridge Ancient History, 1st edition: vols 7 and 8 (Cambridge, 1928, 1930): B.L. Hallward's classic accounts of all three Punic Wars, still worthwhile.

The Cambridge Ancient History, 2nd edition: vol. 7 part 2, and vol. 8 (both: Cambridge, 1989): modern summaries of the Punic Wars, and accounts of the Roman and Carthaginian background; extensive bibliographies.

Caven, B., *The Punic Wars* (London, 1980): a good short study; no footnotes.

Connolly, P., *Greece and Rome at War* (London and New York, 1981): a vivid, brilliantly illustrated, sometimes controversial description and analysis of Greek and Roman war-making; also discusses the Carthaginian armies and navy, with special treatment of Hannibal's War.

Daly, G., *Cannae: the Experience of Battle* (London and New York, 2003): thorough analysis of the rival military systems and of the 'face of battle' at Cannae.

De Beer, Sir G., *Hannibal's March* (London, 1967): a famous study of the evidence for Hannibal's route to Italy, arguing for the Durance valley and the Col de la Traversette.

Goldsworthy, A., *The Punic Wars* (London, 2000; reissued in paperback as *The Fall of Carthage: the Punic Wars*, 2003): an up-to-date and perceptive narrative, chiefly of the military events of the wars.

Hackett, Sir J. (ed.), *Warfare in the Ancient World* (London, 1989): collection of chapters by specialists on warfare from Sumeria to the fall of Rome, with many illustrations.

Hoyos, B.D., *Unplanned Wars: the Origins of the First and Second Punic Wars* (Berlin and New York, 1998): analyses why the first two wars occurred, with stress on miscalculation and mutual bluffing, and assessment of Hannibal's contribution to the outbreak of the Second.

Hoyos, D., *Hannibal's Dynasty: Power and Politics in the Western Mediterranean, 247–183 BC* (London and New York, 2003; paperback, with maps, 2005): studies the rise and predominance of the Barcid leaders at Carthage, their policies in peace and war, and the aftermath of their dominance; extensive analysis of Hannibal's own career and achievements.

Lancel, S., *Carthage: a History* (English translation: London, 1995): a vividly up-to-date account of the city and its fortunes, with many illustrations and maps, by a leading historical archaeologist.

Lancel, S., *Hannibal* (English tr.: London, 1999): perceptive, humane and engrossing biography, with numerous illustrations.

Lazenby, J., *Hannibal's War: a Military History* (Warminster, 1978): a thorough and brilliant study, well illustrated and with plentiful maps.

Lazenby, J., *The First Punic War: a Military History* (London, 1995): a detailed and readable account which helps to place the later war in context.

Picard, G.C., *Daily Life at Carthage in the Time of Hannibal* (English tr.: London, 1964): fascinating description not just of everyday living but also of the culture, economy and religious life of third-century BC Carthage.

Picard, G.C. and Picard, Colette, *The Life and Death of Carthage* (London, 1968): a stimulating, often controversial biography of the city and its civilisation, with extensive treatment of Hannibal's times; lavish illustrations.

Proctor, Sir D., *Hannibal's March in History* (Oxford, 1971): the best study, with controversial conclusions, of the chronology and topography; extremely readable (unfortunately out of print, but available in many libraries).

Scullard, H.H., *The Elephant in the Greek and Roman World* (London, 1974): enlightening on the rôle of elephants in the Punic as well as other wars.

Scullard, H.H., *Scipio Africanus: Soldier and Politician* (London, 1970): a judicious, fairly compact biography, with personal knowledge of the terrains, and plentiful maps and illustrations.

Thiel, J.H., *Studies on the History of Roman Sea-Power in Republican Times* (Amsterdam, 1946): by a naval specialist and ancient historian, and still the only detailed study of its topic; over half is devoted to the Second Punic War.

Toynbee, A.J., *Hannibal's Legacy*, 2 vols (Oxford, 1965): a magisterial study of the Hannibalic War's effects on the economy, society and culture of Rome and Italy, still of major importance although many of its conclusions have been challenged.

Walbank, F.W., *A Historical Commentary on Polybius*, 3 vols (Oxford, 1957, 1967, 1979): the most important guide to and discussion of Polybius' work and its contents; knowledge of Greek is not essential, though useful.

Warmington, B.H., *Carthage* (Harmondsworth, 1964): concise history of the city-state, especially its politics and wars.

The most important recent studies of Hannibal are in German, by J. Seibert: *Forschungen zu Hannibal* [Studies on Hannibal] and *Hannibal* (both Darmstadt, 1993). The most monumental, and still a vital, account of the Second Punic War is by G. de Sanctis, *Storia dei Romani*, vol. 3 part 2 (1st edition, 1916; 2nd edition, Florence, 1968).

NOTES

1. On Carthage's artificial ports see, for example, S. Lancel, *Carthage: a History*, 172–88.
2. Diodorus 20.8.3–4.
3. Silius, *Punica* 1.72–6 (72–3 translated) and 87–8.
4. Polybius 3.11; Livy 21.1. Later in his history, Livy gives the Polybian version (35.19).
5. Silius, *Punica* 3.97–107 (Imilce), 4.763–829 (their son).
6. Fabius Pictor's claims: Polybius 3.8.
7. Livy 39.52.
8. Polybius 9.22.
9. Cicero, *De Divinatione* 1.49 (citing Silenus).
10. Polybius 3.55; Livy 21.37; Vitruvius 8.3.19.
11. Polybius 3.96.
12. Livy 22.2.
13. Polybius 3.88.
14. Plutarch, *Fabius* 15.
15. Livy 22.51 (author's tr.). Cato's version had Hannibal change his mind next day, only for Maharbal to tell him brusquely it was already too late.
16. Livy 22.58.
17. Livy 23.42.
18. Livy 23.2.
19. Polybius 7.9 (Shuckburgh's tr., slightly adapted).
20. Polybius 5.104 (speech of Agelaus of Naupactus).
21. Livy 21.4; Dio, fragment 54; Pliny the Elder, *Natural History* 3.103; Appian, *Hannibalica* 43.
22. Appian, *Libyca* 63 and 134.
23. Polybius 9.3–4.

24. Polybius 9.4.
25. Livy 27.16; Plutarch, *Fabius* 23.
26. Livy 27.27; Plutarch, *Marcellus* 9.
27. Livy 27.51.
28. Livy 30.23.
29. Pol. 15.6–8.
30. Appian, *Civil Wars* 3.68.279–81.
31. Livy 30.37.
32. Victor, *Caesars* 37.
33. Livy 30.44 (abbreviated).
34. Livy 33.46 (author's tr.).
35. On the *quartier Hannibal*, see Lancel, *Carthage* 156–62.
36. Livy 33.47 (author's tr.).
37. Livy, ibid.
38. Juvenal 10.159–62.
39. Livy 35.14 (author's tr.).
40. Plutarch, *Lucullus* 31; Strabo, *Geography* 11.14.6, p. 528.
41. Nepos, *Hannibal* 9.
42. Pliny the Elder, *Natural History* 5.148.
43. Livy 39.51.
44. Juvenal 10.163–6.
45. Cicero, *De Finibus* 4.9.22; *Philippics* 1.5.11.
46. Polybius 11.19.
47. Livy 22.53.
48. Polybius 9.22.

INDEX

Frequently mentioned names are not indexed